THE STRIPPED-DOWN GUIDE TO CONTENT MARKETING

Copyright © 2022 John Egan

All rights reserved. No part of this publication may be reproduced, distributed, or transmitted in any form or by any means, including photocopying, recording, or other electronic or mechanical methods, without the prior written permission of the publisher, except in the case of brief quotations embodied in critical reviews and certain other noncommercial uses permitted by copyright law. For permission requests, write to the publisher, addressed "Attention: Permissions Coordinator," at the address below.

ISBN: 979-8-9862582-0-1 (ebook)
ISBN: 979-8-218-00334-0 (paperback)
ISBN: 979-8-9862582-1-8 (hardcover)

Ordering Information:
Special discounts are available on quantity purchases by corporations, associations, and others. For details, contact johneganaustin@gmail.com or visit johnegan.net.

THE STRIPPED-DOWN GUIDE TO CONTENT MARKETING

JOHN EGAN

TABLE OF CONTENTS

STRIPPING IT DOWN: WHAT IS CONTENT MARKETING?

YOU'VE SEEN WHAT your competitors are doing and how their businesses have been thrust forward with great content marketing. But you aren't out to simply copy them. Your company has a particular niche and loyal customers who crave its products and services, or maybe you've just started your business. Regardless of your business's background, you're well aware that if you craft content messages specifically for your market, word will spread to new customers. But the big question persists: How can you succeed at content marketing? Let me assure you that you have purchased the correct guide. I will answer that question and more. But first, I want to start at the beginning, at the foundation. It's a must.

What is content marketing? And when did it become

so popular?

When I was studying journalism at the University of Kansas—go Jayhawks!—the students and the professors had no clue what content marketing was. It existed at the time, back in the 1980s, but it wasn't called content marketing. We probably would have dismissed it as advertising, which was a dirty word to us hardcore journalism folks.

con•tent mar•ket•ing

noun

content marketing involves creating and sharing relevant, valuable, high-quality content—such as blog posts, e-books, and white papers—that is aimed at attracting, educating, informing, enlightening, and retaining current and potential members of your audience.

One company, however, inadvertently discovered the vitality of content marketing way back in 1895 (although it probably didn't realize at the time what it had discovered). John Deere, the company widely recognized for its trademark green and yellow farm equipment, was one of the first companies to employ—and find great success with—what's now called content marketing.[1] No, it didn't invent social media. It used time-tested print media and introduced its own magazine, *The Furrow,* as "A Journal for the American Farmer."[2] John Deere inherently knew what its customers wanted and needed—and delivered it.

In fact, the company still publishes the magazine, produced by an eight-member editorial team, and it has evolved from a quarterly to a monthly publication. Today, there's even a John

Deere podcast, *On Life & Land*.[3] A pleasant surprise to me is that *The Furrow* originates from the John Deere Ag Marketing Center in my hometown of Olathe, Kansas.

At the outset, the magazine concentrated on subjects such as farming challenges and agricultural trends. Recent topics covered in the magazine—which has been dubbed the "agrarian version of *Rolling Stone*"[4]—include urban agriculture, alternative crops, profit-eating weeds, and bee "vectoring."

Produced in more than 20 languages, the magazine enjoys distribution of about two million in over 100 countries;[5] most readers are John Deere customers.[6] Now as then, *The Furrow* strives to build brand loyalty in a subtle, non-"salesy" way. Ultimately, of course, John Deere wants the magazine's readers to buy its farm equipment.[7]

The creation of the publication was a brilliant marketing move. "Before *The Furrow* hit the scene, farmers didn't have an organized place to see their challenges, hopes, and community-specific knowledge reflected at them. What *The Furrow* got so right from the get-go is that it addressed farmers' pain points," according to Express Writers. "By offering actionable information about how to cope with difficult farming situations and address various issues in the community," Express Writers notes, "*The Furrow* proved it understood its audience. What's more, it offered truly valuable information that increased the quality of their lives."[8]

That information has yielded impressive results. At Content Marketing World 2014, David Jones, then editor of *The Furrow*, reported that:

→ One-third of readers bought John Deere products as a

result of reading *The Furrow*.

→ 90 percent of readers said *The Furrow* was their sole source of industry information.[9]

While John Deere was (and is) a pioneer in the field, it's hardly the only company that engaged in content marketing well before it became mainstream. The MarTech website points out that tire manufacturer Michelin (*The Michelin Guide*), gelatin brand Jell-O (recipe books), engineering firm Burns & McDonnell (*BenchMark* magazine), and retailer Sears (radio show) were early innovators in content marketing.

But it's John Deere that deserves credit for truly plowing the content marketing territory. "The content featured in *The Furrow* was educational, and it focused on teaching farmers how to be more fruitful business owners—a quintessential example of content marketing," MarTech notes.

Decades after I graduated from KU and even more decades after John Deere launched *The Furrow*, I would not only learn what content marketing is but also make a living in content marketing. It's amazing to ponder how big the global content marketing industry has become since its birth during the presidency of Grover Cleveland.

The Furrow is just one of many success stories in the global content marketing industry, which is estimated to exceed $107.5 billion by 2026, up from nearly $36.8 billion in 2018.[10] That near tripling represents a hell of a lot of content being cranked out by the likes of corporate giants such as Amazon and Coca-Cola, not to mention software start-ups, schools, healthcare systems, banks, and everything in between.

But it's important to recognize that content marketing is not advertising. It's not PR. It's not straight-up marketing. It's producing and sharing content, in an array of forms, that resonates with your target audience. I like to think of it as marketing infused with the DNA of journalism.

Content marketing also is not a one-size-fits-all concept. It must be tailored to your organization's needs and goals (or at least it *should* be). What works for a company like e-commerce behemoth Amazon assuredly won't work for beverage titan Coca-Cola.

My content marketing strategy work, for instance, at self-storage marketplace SpareFoot versus my work at outdoor services marketplace LawnStarter bears this knowledge out. While both start-ups cater to B2C (business to consumer) and B2B (business to business) customers, their audiences are vastly different. For example, content about decluttering plays well to the SpareFoot audience; it doesn't appeal much to the LawnStarter audience, which is far more interested in how to maintain a green lawn.

The Naked Truth About Content Marketing

Let's list the main elements of content marketing:

Successful content marketing is not a rigidly defined concept.[11] It can and should be molded to the needs and goals of your organization.

→ Successful content marketing is not a one-time project. It must be carried out and measured consistently.

→ Successful content marketing does not require a multimillion-dollar budget.

"One of the key traits of a great content marketing [strategy] is having an ability to continually problem-solve and learn new things," according to the Digital Marketing Institute. "Content marketing isn't rocket science, but it does take some patience, creativity and an analytical outlook."[12]

It also takes a clear understanding of your target audience. Executing a great content marketing strategy demands creation of engaging content—content that they crave, content that they can't wait to eat up, content that they love sharing with their friends, relatives, and colleagues.[13]

Your Content Marketing Should Be as Agile as a Gymnast

Great content marketing also requires agility. And perhaps no other era in modern history has highlighted the need for agility in content marketing than has the coronavirus pandemic.

A prime example of pandemic-era agility comes courtesy of Walgreens, the massive drugstore chain. Following the onset of the pandemic, Walgreens modified its "Ask a Pharmacist" series on YouTube by creating short videos that answered customers' common questions about COVID-19.[14][15] This service provided an immediate solution to the need for reliable information related to the pandemic.

Walgreens could have maintained the status quo of its content calendar for its "Ask a Pharmacist" series but smartly pivoted to meet the demand for up-to-date COVID-19 information, and the switch made sense. Staying on the same track as had been laid out before the pandemic could have come off as tone-deaf, especially for a major healthcare brand.

It does not take a pandemic to fine-tune your content marketing strategy, though. For example, you may need to change course if your business enters a new geographic or product market. Or a shift may be in order because of technological changes, such as the rise of mobile devices; the adjustment may include mobile-friendly updates of your organization's website, social media presence, or email campaigns.[16]

Indeed, innovative variations keep a business's face fresh in the barrage of available content. Luxury fashion and beauty brand Burberry deserves credit for a particularly creative way to embrace mobile content marketing. To promote its beauty products, Burberry developed a campaign called Burberry Kisses. Via a mobile app, a user could press their lips to the screen and send a digital kiss to someone. The campaign even let the user track a digital kiss through Google Street View and Google Maps.[17]

Just as Walgreens pivoted during the pandemic and Burberry embraced mobile marketing, your brand can—and should—be agile, no matter how young or old your brand is. After all, Germany's Johanna Quass was still doing a gymnastics routine in 2021 at age 95. Experiment with ways that your brand can vault ahead in content marketing by being as agile as Johanna Quass. Don't fear falling off the balance beam.

Successful Content Marketing Is Not a One-and-Done Project

Unfortunately, you cannot simply publish a few blog posts and expect folks to flock to your content (and get more familiar with your brand). If you want your content marketing to resonate and actually generate results, you must commit to a long-term strategy that can be paired with a delivery cadence.

Cadence refers to "the pattern of the content—meaning it includes the number of marketing emails/blogs/case studies/texts/calls sent, the spacing between them, the actual content sent, and the audience that's receiving and consuming…what you are sending," according to Olivia Gochnour, the head of people operations at Tiled,[18] whose technology enables creation of multimedia experiences.

So, good content marketing is not just one mode. Both strategy and cadence align with consistency, which can help you build credibility, trust, and reputation. Of course, all of those outcomes are important, but don't underestimate strategy and consistency in generating revenue, too. According to Alex DiRenzo from Shutterstock, the provider of stock photos, brands that maintain content consistency see a 23 percent boost in revenue. Surprisingly, though, brands are not consistent when it comes to consistency. Half of marketers say 50 percent or less of their content sticks to a consistent brand voice![19]

You have to be "all in" because content marketing strategy, cadence, and consistency can either lift up your brand or drag it down. It's your choice.

You Don't Need a Million Bucks to Succeed in Content Marketing

While content marketing is on track to become a $100 billion global industry, that money is not spread around evenly. At one start-up where I led content marketing strategy, the initial annual budget was in the low six figures. At another start-up where I directed content marketing strategy, the annual budget stood at zero. Yet at both start-ups, we achieved success with our content marketing strategies.

In the chapters ahead, I outline my tried-and-true strategies for content marketing success.

STRIPPING IT DOWN

1. **Aim high.** Seek to share content that resonates with your target audience.

2. **Expose away.** Introduce your audience to multiple types of content: blog posts, infographics, a ranked list (listicle), and so forth.

3. **More isn't better.** Better is better. Go with quality over quantity.

4. **Tailor and then tailor some more.** Mesh your content marketing strategy with your company's goals.

5. **Be agile.** Respond and adapt to your audience's needs.

one

HARVESTING GREAT CONTENT WITH FEW TOOLS

"Content marketing can be challenging—especially when dealing with a 'boring' industry. The truth is that there are no boring industries, just boring content."

—Nayomi Chibana, Visme.co[20]

BORING CONTENT CAN poison your brand. But what if you lack the resources to produce even minimally interesting content? To that, I say: You can generate high-quality content with very little in the way of resources. I know because I've successfully done it.

Let's look at one industry that seems to be uninteresting on the surface and see how it creates engaging content.

The U.S. landscaping services industry rakes in around $100 billion in annual revenue,[21] but it is not exactly a scintillating business sector. Clearly, Americans are obsessed with their lawns—but not necessarily with lawn care. Therefore, attracting media attention for a lawn care start-up is a tough row to hoe.

As editor in chief at LawnStarter, a marketplace for outdoor services, I was tasked with publishing content that would draw interest from readers and media outlets, and ultimately would generate backlinks for the LawnStarter website. One day in 2016, as I was brainstorming content ideas, I happened to stumble upon an observance I'd never heard of—World Naked Gardening Day. It then dawned on me:

How could LawnStarter "newsjack" this pseudo holiday to garner attention for LawnStarter?

Once I pounced on the concept of capitalizing on World Naked Gardening Day, I had to devise a way to drum up a newsworthy angle. That's when it hit me:

Why not rank the best U.S. cities for observing World Naked Gardening Day?

After settling on that idea, we had to determine which data to use to rank U.S. cities. The six statistics we relied on (representing nearly 50 major cities) were:

1. Average high temperature

2. Average percentage of sunshine

3. Average rainfall

4. Average afternoon humidity

5. Average number of cloudy days

6. Average wind speed

Each of the six statistics was weighted evenly and benchmarked against these weather ideals:

→ High temperature of 75 degrees

→ Abundant sunshine

→ Little rainfall

→ Afternoon humidity of 45 percent

→ Few cloudy days

→ Five-mph wind (light breeze)

After crunching the numbers, we arrived at the top 12 cities for observing World Naked Gardening Day. At No. 1 was Miami.[22]

Making Sure the Emperor Has Clothes

With those numbers in hand, we then needed to develop written content and images to make the data come to life.

For the written content, we conducted online research to unearth information about naked gardening, including quotes from the founder of World Naked Gardening Day. Then, to complement the data and the written narrative, we found photos of each of the top 12 cities, as well as safe-for-work pictures of nude gardeners.

We published the World Naked Gardening Day package a few days ahead of the observance to allow time for content promotion.

Exposing the World Naked
Gardening Day to the World

At the core of the outreach strategy was contacting media outlets in the 12 ranked cities to alert them to the World Naked Gardening Day "honor" that had been bestowed upon their communities. We primarily targeted newspapers, TV stations, and radio stations in each market. Reaching out to news outlets is as simple as contacting a reporter or editor by email with your story pitch. Most news outlets are eager to report interesting, relevant information that will draw readers, viewers, and listeners.

We hit the jackpot with our outreach in Miami. The city's daily newspaper, the *Miami Herald*, published a story about the ranking.[23] That story simultaneously was posted online by the nearly 30 other newspapers owned by the *Miami Herald*'s publisher.

In all, more than 120 media outlets reported on the ranking of the best U.S. cities for observing World Naked Gardening Day. That volume included two live TV interviews on World Naked Gardening Day that I conducted with The Weather Channel.[24]

Aside from the widespread media coverage, the LawnStarter blog post itself earned about 1,600 shares on social media.

"The folks at The Weather Channel said it was their favorite story of the year," a LawnStarter ad boasted.[25]

After all was said and done, the World Naked Gardening Day project exceeded expectations, thanks to the dozens of backlinks and media mentions that were secured as well as the two coveted live spots on The Weather Channel.

"The ability to pull television and news coverage from a blog post is the epitome of scrappy marketing," content marketing guru Sujan Patel wrote on Inc.com.[26]

Furthermore, the World Naked Gardening Day campaign elicited citations in articles by Inc.,[27] Forbes, and Keap.com.[28] Here's an excerpt from a Forbes.com Q&A between Patel and my former boss at LawnStarter, co-founder Ryan Farley.

Sujan Patel: I've seen that you guys have gotten all kinds of press, like The Miami Herald and CNN, so you're doing things that are not only scrappy, but things that get people's attention.

I saw several pieces that earned you guys news spots, like reporting on Austin's population growth in your blog, and pulling data from city demographers to do comparisons on water bills across different counties in Texas and Florida. Those all earned you a lot of news coverage, both online and on television.

Ryan Farley: I can't really take credit for that. One of the experts we did hire is our editor, John Egan. He had done this type of thing with insurance and self-storage, and now lawn care. He's amazed me in that he has turned our lawn care blog into something that's being referenced as a news source.[29]

Cultivating a Content Marketing Garden with Few Tools

Now, you might think that LawnStarter earmarked hundreds or even thousands of dollars for the successful World Naked Gardening Day campaign. Think again. We carried out the campaign with zero dollars. Zero. I researched the piece, wrote the piece, and pitched the piece to media outlets, although I did get a data-crunching assist from other members of the marketing team. It was largely a solo endeavor, though. To come up with contact information for pitching, I scoured the internet for names and email addresses of reporters, editors, and other media folks. You can also buy media lists, but I went down the DIY path since we had no money for outreach efforts.

Throughout my tenure at LawnStarter, not a single penny was budgeted for content marketing beyond salaries for me and our search engine optimization (SEO) specialist (see Chapter 3 for specifics on SEO and its importance). Other than that investment, we had no pot of money to dip into for writing or PR or social media or anything else. LawnStarter executed content marketing initiatives with not even a shoestring budget (and no shoes, to boot).

According to *Forbes*, a start-up should aim to spend 25-30 percent of its marketing budget on content marketing.[30] To me, that seems like a reasonable sum. For a start-up with $500,000 in annual revenue, that formula would lead to a content marketing budget of $6,250 to $15,000.

Check out these statistics. In a survey conducted by the Content Marketing Institute, 36 percent of B2B marketers reported having an annual content marketing budget in 2019 of less than $100,000. The average was $185,000. On the other end of the spectrum, 18 percent reported having no budget for content marketing.[31]

Not surprisingly, B2B marketers that spent the most money on content marketing reported achieving the most success, while B2B marketers that spent the least on content marketing achieved the least success.[32]

Boy, I wish I'd had an annual budget of even $3,000 for content marketing at LawnStarter. Alas, that wasn't possible.

As my experience at LawnStarter demonstrates, however,

you need not spend any money on content marketing to realize success. But I wonder how much more success we could have enjoyed if we'd had a dedicated budget for content marketing. The bottom line here is: You don't need money to gain traction with content marketing, but it sure does help.

Beyond the Bare Necessities

Looking back, I consider the World Naked Gardening Day campaign to be the crowning achievement of LawnStarter's content marketing efforts during my tenure there (2015-2017). Yet, you can't pin success on a single initiative. When your success as a content marketer is measured almost exclusively by the volume of backlinks secured, a lone campaign like World Naked Gardening Day won't cut it.

So, how do you regularly crank out high-quality, eyeball-attracting content with no budget, no external resources, and very few internal resources?

First off, you work your butt off. I constantly combed the internet for ideas tied directly to lawn care or that were lawn care-adjacent (such as data about people's homes and home lots). In particular, I looked for snippets of information that alone or combined with other data could be transformed into a listicle or an infographic.

That approach generated pieces of content like "America's Love Affair With Bedrooms and Bathrooms [Infographic],"[33] "Kansas City Metro Leads the Way for Big Home Lots,"[34] and "The 14 Most Maxed-Out Metros for Housing Debt."[35] Or I hunted for places like sports stadiums that we could rank. That idea produced content like "The 9 Finest Grass Fields in

Minor League Baseball,"[36] "Turf Battle in the NFL: Natural vs. Artificial"[37] (a rundown of pro-football stadiums with natural and artificial turf), and "Report Card: The 14 Most Picturesque High School Campuses in the U.S."[38]

Overall, I spent a ton of time sifting through data from the U.S. Census Bureau or exploring photos on Google to come up with concepts for content marketing pieces and then developing pieces of content that I believed would click with media outlets and consumers (consumers who, we hoped, would share our posts on social media).

After a while, a pattern emerged. Rankings that focused on various aspects of major metro areas and on the "prettiest fill-in-the-blank" (stadiums, fountains, and so forth) generally delivered gold. We generated lists tied to colleges, private colleges, two-year colleges, high schools, private high schools… you get the picture. We put out content regarding population growth, housing types, and other topics connected to the home.

The success of the rankings and the "prettiest" content highlighted a common thread among humans: We take pride in our communities and our schools. If a ranking or a piece of "prettiest" content put a community or school in a positive light, media outlets often published stories about them and locals frequently shared the love on social media (particularly Facebook). As always, the objective was to garner backlinks to content on the LawnStarter site from high-quality websites (such as sites for reputable media outlets) in order to raise our Google domain authority.

As explained by BigCommerce, whose technology helps e-commerce merchants, domain authority "is a search engine ranking score that gives a measure of how successful a site is when it comes to search engine results."[39] The higher the score, the more authoritative a site is viewed as being and the higher a site may appear in Google search results. When you're engaged in content marketing, you soon realize that Google is a god-like entity when it comes to success or failure online.

Adapting to Survive and Thrive

So, other than working your butt off, how do you make this magic happen when you have little to nothing in terms of a content marketing budget? You adapt.

Before joining LawnStarter, I knew nothing about designing an infographic or crunching data in a spreadsheet. In fact, I was allergic to Excel spreadsheets pre-LawnStarter—didn't want to have a thing to do with them.

Hey, I'm a word guy, not a numbers guy. That's why I studied journalism, not math. But to create content that would draw attention, I had to overcome my lack of knowledge about infographic design and had to get over my fear of Excel.

While I didn't bear the entire infographic-designing and data-crunching burden at LawnStarter, I did need to pull my weight. So, with an assist from colleagues, I jumped into the deep end of the infographic and data pool.

Just as someone needs a teacher to learn how to swim, I needed teachers to guide me regarding infographics and data-crunching. For me, those teachers primarily were growth marketers Jake Lane and Michael Berliner. Jake lent his knowledge of infographics, and Michael contributed his data-wrangling expertise. Without them, I would have been flailing. The experience taught me that it's impossible to successfully create and distribute content without the support of your colleagues; if you don't have colleagues to lean on, try turning to LinkedIn, Facebook groups, webinars, and similar resources. Jake and Michael supplied their know-how on an as-needed basis, and their know-how gave me the confidence to wade deeper and deeper into the often-choppy waters of infographics and data-wrangling. There was no need for it to be a solo swim.

Sure, I couldn't glide through the pool like Olympic champion Michael Phelps in terms of infographics and data. But I didn't have to turn in a medal-winning performance, either; I just needed to keep my head above water. In the end, we made a splash.

That element of my LawnStarter experience reinforced that we are capable of accomplishing much more than our mind sometimes tells us we can. If I hadn't beat back my mental demons about infographics and spreadsheets, I would have fallen short of achieving LawnStarter's content marketing goals—and would have missed out on a great opportunity to improve my skill set.

Embrace Falling Flat on Your Face (or Your Butt)

In addition to working your butt off and adapting to your environment, what else feeds into successful content marketing when your organization lacks adequate resources? Don't fear failure. You must put content out into the universe. While not every piece of content you produce will be a winner like the World Naked Gardening Day package was, don't be intimidated.

I saw plenty of duds along the way. One that comes to

mind is an infographic I assembled about the windy weather in Tallahassee, Florida.[40] The data was solid. The infographic was attractive. But we gained no traction with the infographic being shared on social media or being picked up by media outlets.

Why did the infographic flop? I'm not entirely sure of the answer, but I can hazard a couple of guesses. One possibility: Tallahassee is a small market with few media outlets, so the pool of targets for sharing on social media and building links was shallow. Another possibility: The infographic narrowly targeted Tallahassee, meaning Tallahassee would be the only market interested in this content. As a result, we had fewer opportunities to tap into an audience for the infographic.

So, what can we take away from the Tallahassee flop? Aside from broadening the appeal of a piece of content, the conclusion that stands out most is that you should figure out why the content didn't get traction, strive to not let the same dud happen again, and move on.

At SpareFoot, the self-storage start-up where I worked before LawnStarter, one of the core values I remember well is this: Fail quickly.

All of the media outreach in the world won't bear fruit if a piece of content doesn't fuel interest on the part of reporters and editors. It may not be your fault. Perhaps a reporter or editor you pitched ignored your email or deleted your email or simply rejected your pitch. Such an outcome very well could occur over and over again with a single piece of content. But you can't feel dejected, and you can't repeatedly nag reporters and editors (for fear of pissing them off); you must give up sooner rather than later and shift to other content marketing efforts.

Looking at it another way, perhaps the piece of content turned out to be low-quality. You think it's awesome, but your potential audience gives it a massive thumbs-down. Whenever a piece of content flops, for whatever reason, it's vital to fail quickly. In other words, don't obsess over the failed piece of content and don't wear it like an albatross. Rather, take the lessons learned from the poorly performing content and march ahead.

I would argue that a situation like that isn't entirely a failure, as you can always learn from your "mistakes." Just as you "rinse and repeat" with top-notch content, you must "rinse and ditch" with content that doesn't gain traction.

Let's Get Naked and Get Ready for Success

One of my takeaways from World Naked Garden Day revolves around success: You've got to be ready for it. When The Weather Channel contacted us and asked to schedule not one but two live shots on World Naked Gardening Day, I had to devise a plan for what I wanted to convey on the air. After all, you have a short window of time to get your message across on live TV. Translation: Be prepared for opportunities that unexpectedly come your way. We would have been extremely foolish to be unprepared and to pass up two live shots on The Weather Channel. Talk about exposure (pun intended)!

Thankfully, the on-air messaging was clear: Focus on World Naked Gardening Day, not on LawnStarter. Yes, The Weather Channel anchors mentioned LawnStarter, and that was a victory all on its own. Yet, it would have been foolish to treat The Weather Channel segments like infomercials for LawnStarter. The anchors weren't interested in plugging LawnStarter, and the audience didn't care about our company. My sole purpose for appearing on these segments was to discuss World Naked Gardening Day. Period. The best I could hope for was that the segments would boost awareness of the LawnStarter brand and would potentially lead to more media exposure. As far as I can tell, we accomplished that.

The World Naked Gardening Day campaign also underscores the importance of keeping an eye on what works and what doesn't. While I can't recall every piece of content that flopped, I did pick up enough from each experience to make tweaks in future content creation and promotion. At the same time, I realized that other failures would be on the horizon. Similarly, I sought to copy what did work and repeat it.

Although World Naked Gardening Day is observed just once a year, LawnStarter continues to publish an annual list of the best places to observe World Naked Gardening Day. As the folks at LawnStarter have learned, sexy sells—or at least gardening in the buff does. While the lawn care industry may be outwardly boring, naked gardening is anything but.

And here, the naked truth is that you can create plenty of outstanding content that generates traffic without relying on a box overflowing with tools. You must adopt the mindset that no matter how big or small your organization is and no matter how few tools you have, you can succeed at content marketing. Just remember to fail quickly if something doesn't work—rather than tilling the same ground over and over—and repeat what does work. Armed with that kind of attitude, your efforts can repeatedly bear fruit.

STRIPPING IT DOWN

1. **Adopt a scrappy mindset.** You can create high-quality, impactful content without a big budget. Money shouldn't be the driving factor.

2. **Overcome your fears.** If you don't possess the skills that you need to execute your content marketing strategy, learn them. Keep in mind that you don't need to be an expert at a skill—you simply must do it well.

3. **Get comfortable with failure.** Not every piece of content you produce will be a winner. Learn from the experience and move on quickly.

4. **Repeat what works.** You'll likely stumble on a formula that consistently delivers. Stick to that formula; don't deviate from it.

5. **Prepare for success.** The success of a piece of content may wildly exceed your expectations. Be ready to seize on opportunities to capitalize on that success.

two

PLANTING YOUR STAKE
IN THE GROUND

IN 2013, THE opportunity arose for me to go from leading content marketing strategy for a collection of insurance websites to leading content marketing strategy for a pair of self-storage websites. Neither insurance nor self-storage is sexy. Trust me—those topics can be as dry as South America's Atacama Desert, the driest place on Earth.

I ended up accepting the content marketing role at SpareFoot, a self-storage marketplace now under the Storable corporate umbrella.[41] Having worked in the unsexy insurance sector, I was undeterred by working in the equally unsexy self-storage sector. And, as it turned out, the self-storage sector supplied lots of fertile ground for storytelling—storytelling that would help build the authority of the SpareFoot brand.

What really excited me about joining SpareFoot was the chance—as my SpareFoot boss, Brian Megless, summed up at the time—to craft "professional and industry-leading content." Brian hoped to replicate the editorial success of another Austin-based company, CreditCards.com[42] (a corporate sister of Bankrate Insurance,[43] where I worked when SpareFoot extended the job offer).[44] Brian told me that SpareFoot sought "to improve the quantity and quality of the content we create and get better and more effective at distributing it."

Brian further explained that generating industry-leading content was "a must-have" to establish SpareFoot as the go-to source for all things self-storage. That connection was critical, he said, to boosting earned media (as opposed to paid media) and accumulating more high-quality, authoritative backlinks to SpareFoot.com and SelfStorage.com. The result, Brian said, would be to drive more direct and organic web traffic for the demand side of the business (self-storage renters) as well as to the supply side of the business (self-storage facility owners and operators).

From Opportunity to Operations

At the core of this effort: Build the authority of the SpareFoot brand, a trailblazing brand that early on met with a fair amount of skepticism in self-storage circles. Some owners and operators in the industry viewed SpareFoot as an upstart that would steal business from them. We needed to rise above that skepticism with killer content.

We settled on positioning the SpareFoot blog as mostly a consumer hub for advice about moving and organizing, two key drivers of self-storage demand. Meanwhile, the SelfStorage.com blog, called The Storage Facilitator, would continue to educate and inform self-storage owners and operators.

We also added a third blog, The SpareFoot Storage Beat. This new blog would report on what now is a roughly $40 billion industry in the U.S.[45] The blog would feature news about self-storage acquisition and development activity ("Forecast: Self-Storage Revenue to Pass $30B in 2018"[46] and "Storage operators regroup after hurricanes strike"[47] are just two examples) along with earnings updates for the handful of publicly traded self-storage real estate investment trusts (REITs).

A linchpin for the SpareFoot Storage Beat would be hiring a full-time reporter who would cover the self-storage industry just as a commercial real estate reporter might. We wound up bringing aboard Al Harris, a reporter from Richmond, Virginia,[48] with experience in commercial real estate. (He took my place as editor at SpareFoot after I departed for LawnStarter in 2015.)

With Al's hiring, we essentially set up a newsroom dedicated to covering an industry that received scant notice from traditional media, except the regular stories about Americans and their junk. Our news operation aimed to dig into the self-storage industry beyond the ubiquitous press releases. Let me emphasize that we approached reporting on the self-storage sector with the same rigor that any traditional news operation would. A brand need not toss aside journalistic standards when creating content; if anything, a brand should adhere to journalistic standards when creating content.

Fielding a Team of Freelancers

Al and I couldn't have adequately produced content for three websites on our own. So, I went about assembling a stable of solid freelance writers to create blog posts that would appeal to both self-storage consumers and self-storage professionals. We also leaned heavily on infographics, designed by an outside firm, as a secondary storytelling tool. Additionally, we came up with novel ways to drum up publicity for SpareFoot, such as inventing a holiday called National Moving Day (more on that later).[49]

While it's possible to successfully carry out a content marketing strategy with no budget and no outside resources, it certainly can be overwhelming. It's especially hard to do so when you're running more than one website. If you're spread too thin, quality will almost certainly suffer.

That's why it was vital for SpareFoot to outsource much of the content creation to freelancers. But not just any freelancers. Talented freelancers with a proven track record who expected—and deserved—more than a measly 10 cents per word for blog posts. It's my belief that you get what you pay for.

So, if you pay 10 cents a word for a blog post, you'll likely be saddled with editing and rewriting some crappy copy. However, if you pay an attractive rate (either on a per-word or flat-fee basis), you'll attract freelancers whose work doesn't need the kind of complicated overhaul that a notoriously tough-to-fix Audi 8 would require.

I went about recruiting freelancers mostly by dipping into the talent pool I'd used as the leader of content marketing strategy at Bankrate Insurance. Also, I scoured LinkedIn for prospective freelance writers, sifted through my professional contacts, and considered freelancers who worked with websites I'd previously written for (like National Real Estate Investor,[50] now known as Wealth Management Real Estate).[51] That effort went a long way toward ensuring SpareFoot could consistently generate high-quality content.

Another consideration if you're drafting freelancers for your content marketing team: Be sure to vet their qualifications, and don't be afraid to let them go if they're not delivering the goods. A well-rounded group of freelancers can be a huge asset, but a few less-than-stellar freelancers can eat up valuable time, gobble up precious dollars, and drag down your content marketing efforts.

Eyeing Infographics

Early on in my content marketing career, I admired the work of a particular residential real estate website. In fact, I went so far as to chat with one of Movoto's editors about their recipe for success. It wasn't complicated: Movoto exploited the weaknesses of its competitors. That strategy catapulted Movoto from 2,000 monthly blog visits to 18 million blog visits over the course of two years.[52]

Part of the strategy involved producing infographics like the one from 2014 that assigned a value to the fictional restaurant on the Fox TV series *Bob's Burgers*. HubSpot, a producer of content marketing software, lauded the effort, noting that "Movoto successfully took a pop culture topic—the hit television show *Bob's Burgers*—and used their expertise to create a clever, relevant, and shareable infographic about it."[53]

Now, I love a good infographic. But I truly love the written word. As a kid, I devoured books and newspapers. Over the course of my career as a newspaper reporter and editor, I may have spit out more words than you'll find in the famously (or infamously) long novel *War and Peace*, weighing in at a hefty

587,287 words.

That being said, not everyone is the voracious reader that I am. Many of us are primarily visual learners. In fact, it's estimated that 65 percent of us fall into the visual-learning category.[54] The power of visual learning is hard to deny; research shows that people remember just 10 percent of the information they hear, yet 65 percent recall the information they spot in a data visualization.[55]

Simply put, the blog for Easelly, which offers an infographic-making tool, notes that "your brain loves looking at pictures."[56] Content marketing platform Semrush emphasizes that from an SEO viewpoint, the infographic remains one of the most effective methods for building backlinks to your website.[57]

"Infographics are effective because they combine the written word with visual elements to pack big ideas into small spaces," according to the Miss Details design and branding agency. "Presenting information in such a compelling fashion encourages visitors to spend time on your site, consuming and sharing more of your content."[58]

Before I joined SpareFoot, I had turned to infographics to supplement our content strategy at Bankrate Insurance. We enlisted an infographic design agency called NowSourcing, led by infographics guru Brian Wallace, to create our infographics.[59]

To save money, we conducted the research on our own and then handed over the data to NowSourcing. The firm almost magically created our infographics and then sought places to publish them (so we could benefit from high-quality backlinks). At SpareFoot, I once again called on the talents of NowSourcing for help with infographics. We also depended on our amazing

SEO team at SpareFoot for in-house development of keywords for some of our infographics.

The one SpareFoot infographic success story that I most vividly remember is the infographic we published about whether Austin, Texas, or Portland, Oregon, is the weirder city.[60] Both places revel in their weird vibes, but we set out to settle the debate once and for all. The infographic certainly had nothing to do with self-storage, but both Austin and Portland are big self-storage markets where rentals are available on the SpareFoot platform. (In case you're wondering, Portland won the weirdness battle.)

For this infographic, I researched factors that could be viewed as indicators of weirdness. To determine the weirdest city, we considered previously published rankings on such topics as the best cities for hipsters, the most tattooed cities, and the most pot-friendly cities. SpareFoot SEO specialist Brian Shreckengast designed the infographic.[61]

We then pitched the infographic to media outlets in Austin and Portland. Outlets in Portland pounced on the infographic, with the *Portland Business Journal*[62] and *Portland Monthly*[63] among those citing (and linking to) the infographic in articles. Furthermore, the infographic amassed hundreds of pins on Pinterest. A link to the infographic is included in a Wikipedia entry about the "Keep Portland Weird" slogan.[64] And the infographic even warranted a mention in a 2017 article published by the *New Zealand Herald*.[65]

That infographic (and many others I've helped develop) demonstrates the strength of visual learning and the everlasting draw of data visualization.

Since the Austin-Portland infographic appeared in 2014, infographic design has advanced. But what hasn't changed is the storytelling and attention-grabbing clout of infographics. Infographics can be a valuable tool in your content toolbox, as long as they're done right; they must be well-researched and well-designed. If you publish high-quality infographics on your website or on other websites, you stand a good chance of building your brand's visibility and building high-value links to your website.

Drumming Up Publicity

Publicity draws media attention to a product, service, business, or cause. Hollywood stars like Tom Hanks and Tom Cruise rely on publicists to help shape their public image. Of course, publicity is quite different from content marketing. But publicity can complement content marketing by attracting media coverage of the content you generate.

At SpareFoot, I wore a couple of hats. Not only did I oversee content marketing strategy, but I handled public relations. That responsibility meant writing, posting, and distributing press releases, as well as generally pursuing positive media coverage for the company. Part of the time, we leaned on an outside PR firm for assistance. The rest of the time, we tackled PR on our own.

To pump up publicity for SpareFoot, we often focused on matters related to moving, a key motive for renting a self-storage unit. We even went so far as to invent National Moving Day. That day, one day after Memorial Day, traditionally ranks among the busiest days of the year for moving companies and self-storage facilities. Within the self-storage sector, professionals have long referred to this day as Crazy Tuesday.[66] That moniker, however, is an inside-the-industry term and is not consumer-friendly, and consumer-friendly is the name of the game in B2C marketing.

One moving-related PR push, carried out by our outside PR firm, yielded an impressive result just before National Moving Day. We scored a spot in 2014 on the third hour of NBC's popular *Today* morning show. The segment explained how to avoid five common moving mistakes (which appeared nearly word for word on the air and on Today.com based on what I had written for the show's producers).[67] The online article about the moving mistakes even cited a survey SpareFoot had commissioned in 2013 about Americans' moving experiences.

There's no way to determine precisely how much more web traffic or business we gained from the *Today* spot. But it sure gave us bragging rights in terms of landing media coverage.

While you shouldn't expect to always nab a coveted segment on the *Today* show, you still should aim high. To aim high, you must produce high-quality content on a topic that holds broad interest (like moving).

Again, you must be ready if any worthwhile exposure comes calling. Think outside the box. SpareFoot's CEO didn't have a video library of TV appearances, and the folks at the *Today* show weren't wild about my previous TV appearances. So, we wound up hiring a spokeswoman to appear on the *Today* show on behalf of SpareFoot; it was a small price to pay for such massive exposure.

Cultivating positive publicity can certainly augment your content marketing initiatives by, for instance, boosting brand awareness or web traffic. You don't have to hire a publicity pro, though, to achieve such results. With sufficient time and energy, you can successfully take on publicity tasks internally and perhaps earn a spot for your brand on the *Today* show.

Putting It All Together

So, what do freelancers, infographics, and publicity have in common? They all helped SpareFoot bolster its authority among self-storage customers and self-storage professionals. How do I know the authority-building program worked? Here are some nuggets of information that illustrate the program's success:

The Storage Facilitator blog won the award for Best Online Newsroom in Ragan's 2014 PR Daily Awards program.[68]

Among the finalists in the Best Online Newsroom category were Coca-Cola, Adidas, and Nissan.[69] We must have been doing something right if we beat Coca-Cola, Adidas, and Nissan, right?

Not too long after the SpareFoot Storage Beat blog debuted, our CEO received invitations from two Wall Street firms to make presentations about the self-storage sector.

The blog quickly gathered a following, thanks largely to the weekly email newsletter that went out to subscribers. (Newsletters are fantastic tools for distributing your content, by the way.) Without all of that exposure, I doubt SpareFoot would have appeared on Wall Street's radar so soon.

After considerable trial and error, the SEO team managed to get the SpareFoot Storage Beat included in Google News.

That's not easy to accomplish. As SEO consultant Barry Adams explains, you must "jump through quite a few hoops before you get into Google News." But if you successfully jump through those hoops, Google News represents "a really great source of traffic for websites," Adams says. "Once you're in the Google News Index, you can appear in the top stories carousel in Google search results, and that can send a lot of traffic your way."[70]

Moreover, placement in Google News lends credibility to your website. Overall, Google News drives 3-8 percent of total traffic for top web publishers, according to the NewzDash website.[71]

On a stand-alone basis, any one of those accomplishments would fall short of demonstrating that a website has achieved a certain level of authority. But put together, those three examples back up the fact that SpareFoot gained ground in terms of authority. At its core, brand authority builds trust among members of your audience. If your brand lacks sufficient trust from current and potential customers, then your content marketing initiative—and potentially the business itself—could fall flat.

Elevating Brand Authority to a Mount Everest Level

As growth marketing expert Amanda Milligan points out in a post on the website of Moz, a company specializing in SEO, authority earned by a brand paves the way for potential customers (and, I would argue, current customers) to trust and count on your brand.[72] Milligan suggests six ways a brand can develop authority through content:

1. Answer your audience's questions.

2. Create newsworthy reports and studies.

3. Draw on the authority of in-house experts.

4. Highlight reviews, case studies, and other examples of expertise.

5. Team up with other authoritative brands.

6. Share some of your business secrets.[73]

"The very act of investing in content marketing is a big step in building more brand authority. By creating content that's beneficial for your audience, you're demonstrating your own knowledge and utilizing your expertise," Milligan says.[74]

Aside from benefiting your audience, brand authority benefits your organization's position in the Google-verse. As noted by *Search Engine Journal*, Google "prizes authority and is more likely to rank content that oozes with it."[75] (That factor is where search engine optimization comes in.)

The journal goes on to stress that brand authority reigns as the holy grail you attain only after putting in months of hard work to build and consistently maintain your brand reputation. I can attest to that truth. While we achieved short-term wins with our content marketing strategy at SpareFoot, it took lots of labor and consistency to notch long-term gains.

Today, SpareFoot remains what Brian Megless hoped would evolve into the go-to source for all things self-storage. Yes, trade publications and mainstream media outlets dispense information about self-storage. Yet, no one dispenses that information with the same authority that SpareFoot does. SpareFoot continues to commit resources to preserving the brand authority we built, and every brand that immerses itself in content marketing should strive to do the same.

I don't know what SpareFoot's content marketing budget is these days, but when I started out, it was in the low six figures (on top of salaries for the content marketing team). To be sure, not every company can carve out a six-figure budget for content marketing. In the end, though, what truly matters is how much time and energy you expend on your brand's content marketing, not only on how much money you spend.

Fortunately, the folks at SpareFoot realized it would require a healthy financial commitment to plant the company's authority flag in the self-storage ground. I always appreciated that foresight. For your organization, perhaps $10,000 would represent a massive allocation toward content marketing. However, if you seriously expect to build brand authority, you should put some money behind the endeavor. It could end up being the smartest investment your brand ever makes.

Just keep in mind that the dollars you spend on content marketing may not lead directly to generation of leads. Executives at SpareFoot didn't anticipate, let alone demand, that content marketing produce loads of consumers shopping for self-storage space and lots of self-storage owners and operators wanting to list their facilities on the SpareFoot platform.

A return on investment closely tied to lead generation never entered the content marketing picture. Rather, SpareFoot placed a premium on opening the ubiquitous corrugated metal door of a storage unit, if you will, and inviting self-storage consumers and professionals inside to gather knowledge about storage and related subjects. Ultimately, the tactic branded SpareFoot as an industry leader.

You can't buy brand authority. But you can, through a content marketing program, foster brand authority and the trust that goes along with it. As long as your content positions your brand as a valuable source of information tied to your industry, your organization's brand authority should continue to pay dividends. Nevertheless, you should keep in mind that just as you must strive to cultivate brand authority, you must strive to maintain it.

STRIPPING IT DOWN

1. **Act like a journalist.** Adhering to the longtime principles of good journalism can greatly benefit your content. Treat your content the way a stellar news outlet would.

2. **If you're able to hire freelance talent, don't be cheap.** Pay a decent rate. You get what you pay for.

3. **Consider the power of PR.** Publicizing your content via media outlets can raise your brand's visibility and generate more web traffic.

4. **Look beyond leads.** Cultivation of sales leads isn't the only benchmark for content marketing success. Weigh other factors, such as how content is building your brand's authority.

5. **Don't set it and forget it.** Once you've boosted your brand's authority, you must maintain that authority. Otherwise, it could slip away just as quickly as you earned it.

three

THE ABCS OF SEO

AS A WRITER and editor, I've known my ABCs ever since I was a reading and spelling fanatic in elementary school in Kansas.

However, another set of letters—SEO—has been a source of frustration. SEO stands for search engine optimization, and those three letters get thrown around a lot in content marketing circles. Before I entered the content marketing business in 2010, I had no clue what SEO was. I do now, but I'm nowhere near the level of an SEO guru (a description that's frequently bandied about in the SEO sector).

In my content marketing work, I haven't done the heavy lifting in terms of SEO, which helps increase the quality and quantity of traffic coming to a website. Instead, I've depended on SEO specialists or SEO-astute content marketers to guide me when it comes to proper use of keywords. Online, people type in keywords—words or phrases—to find relevant content. For instance, somebody shopping for a car might enter the phrase,

"How to get an auto loan."

Ryan Farley, my SEO-savvy boss at LawnStarter,[76] emphasizes that SEO delivers free (organic) traffic, while search engine marketing (SEM) supplies paid traffic. Furthermore, he says, SEO offers sustained traffic, whereas SEM gives you one-time traffic.

Ryan likens the relationship to buying a place to live (SEO) or renting a place to live (SEM). Buying may be more costly upfront, but it gives you a far better investment over the long haul than renting does. In addition, Ryan asserts, SEO becomes easier over time to carry out, while SEM typically grows more difficult and more expensive to execute.

Still, developing a solid SEO strategy takes time because it's so fiercely competitive.

In a lot of industries, such as real estate, travel, and food, some players have been factoring in SEO for a couple of decades. On top of that advantage, Google—the king of search engines—continually pushes paid ads above organic search results since that's where the company makes money. "But, hey, that's the price you pay for free traffic," Ryan says.

Nonetheless, the value of that free traffic can't be overstated.

When LawnStarter entered the pest control business,[77] the content marketing team devoted three months to creating content related to pest control. Once Google picked up on the fact that LawnStarter was an authority on pest control, it rewarded LawnStarter's website by ranking its content highly in search results.

When your content ranks highly in search results, particularly if your content appears on the first page of search results, your ability to raise the number of people who click on links to your content also goes up.

Ultimately, your SEO strategy rests more on topics and less on keywords. For example, "best lawn mowers" and "top-rated lawn mowers" mean essentially the same thing. So, you should pick keywords that generate the broadest search volume and base your content on them.

"The rest will follow naturally," Ryan says.

Employ tools such as Ahrefs, AnswerThePublic, Clearscope, Google Search Console, Google Trends, and Semrush to do your keyword homework.

"Many times brands believe they know a consumer's pain points just based on surveys or personal experience. SEO can provide insights on what searches are actually important to their target audience that have a decent level of search volume," says Sam Puri, who was one of my go-to SEO guys at Bankrate Insurance.

These days, an assigning editor often supplies the targeted keywords for a piece of content I'm creating as a freelancer. Far be it for me to guess the keywords that my client wants. The bottom line here: Don't leave SEO strategy to quasi-amateurs like me. Put those all-important SEO duties into the hands of the pros, or at least immerse yourself in earning a mini-master's degree in SEO.

If you're SEO-phobic, it's time to get over it.

SEO Phobia and Other Unrelated Fears

For much of my life, I was afraid of heights. But on a trip to Australia in 2008, I overcame that fear even though I hadn't planned to. Everybody else in my tour group was rappelling down cliffs up to 100 feet high and climbing to the top of the Sydney Harbor Bridge, 440 feet above the water. I was the lone holdout. I didn't want to get left out, so I joined my traveling companions on the cliffs and the bridge, and wound up putting my fear of heights behind me. Take the same approach to overcoming any phobia you harbor about SEO.

"Anyone can learn SEO. Seriously. SEO is 100 percent teachable and learnable. Some areas can get very technical, but you can be successful without mastering that side of the house," says Haley Collins, director of operations at GPO (another acronym!), a content marketing agency with offices in Austin and Nashville.

GPO is one of my clients, and Haley is my main contact there. She's far smarter than I am when it comes to SEO, so I've leaned on her (and a couple of other SEO friends) to help me dive into the nitty-gritty of SEO.

Haley explains that if you want your content to be found through organic (unpaid) search, you must be adept at incorporating keywords into your content.

Bottom line: If you fail to artfully weave keywords into your content, your desired audience won't be able to find your content. There's just too much content floating in a vast sea of words, images, and videos. Your keyword-lacking content will simply drown.

Embracing an SEO Strategy Like You Do Your Favorite Aunt

The key to a successful SEO strategy centers on creating content that a potential visitor to your website would find valuable and cutting through the "noise" that Haley mentions. That focus is far more important than trying to trick a search engine like Google into sending traffic to your website.

Therefore, if your website seeks to attract potential insurance customers, your website's content should educate and enlighten them about insurance, not about Lady Gaga. As such, a blog post titled "How to Cut Costs on Car Insurance" would be appropriate and draw potential customers, even though a Lady Gaga piece might bring thousands of visitors.

To help avoid insurance-versus-Lady Gaga debacles, GPO includes a list of keywords in each writing assignment that it sends to a writer. So, when I receive an assignment from GPO, it might include "hissing noise when braking" or "dash lights flickering" as recommended keywords for one of its automotive clients. Those are words or phrases that people might type when they're searching for vehicle-related information online.

GPO expects its writers to be knowledgeable about various subjects but doesn't expect them to be SEO experts. Writers must know how to use SEO tools, apply keywords to achieve the purpose of the content, and naturally weave those keywords into the content. Keywords are aimed at drawing online visitors who are searching for specific information like "how to lose weight fast."

GPO doesn't randomly choose topics—and, therefore, keywords—for its clients. Instead, GPO produces content that targets what its clients' current and future customers are looking for online.

In its assignments, GPO suggests keywords (ones that will help a client rank highly in online searches) and semantically related words. Semantically related keywords are ones that aren't necessary for ranking purposes but should be included to adequately cover a topic. The semantically related keywords appear in other pieces that are chasing after the same primary keywords.

GPO expects all of the suggested keywords to be used at least once in a piece of content. You want to include keywords in the title and first paragraph of a piece of written content, as Haley suggests. You also can feature keywords in subheads within the content.

Regardless of the various places to put keywords, they must appear in your content in order to gain traffic. Otherwise, your chances of appearing on the first and most sought-after page of search results "are slim to none," Haley says.

"Other writers *are* including specific keywords, and they know where to use them," she says. "Don't make Google guess whether you're writing about squeaky brakes or squeaky tires. Be transparent and straightforward in your content intentions. Poetic, fluffy, roundabout language doesn't increase organic traffic or get you coveted placement in search results."

Beware of Keyword Stuffing

Remember that Lady Gaga reference? Well, Lady Gaga would be unable to maintain her poker face if she came across a keyword-stuffed blog post about her meat dress. With apologies to Lady Gaga, here's an example of the wrong way to use keywords:

Lady Gaga wore a meat dress to the 2010 MTV Video Music Awards. The meat dress was made of raw beef. Lady Gaga wore the meat dress to protest the military's "don't ask, don't tell" policy regarding LGBTQ members. Lady Gaga said the meat dress wasn't a statement about animal rights. Years later, the Rock and Roll Hall of Fame displayed Lady Gaga's meat dress. The dried and preserved meat dress subsequently went on display in Las Vegas. Lady Gaga will be forever known for wearing her iconic meat dress.

Even the most diehard of meat lovers (and I love a well-cooked, well-seasoned slice of Texas brisket) should be aghast at that train wreck of a passage. It violates every rule in the SEO rule book.

While keywords are critical to your SEO strategy and, therefore, your content marketing strategy, the Lady Gaga example demonstrates it can be overdone. Not that long ago, some website owners and content creators believed that if they repeated certain keywords "a bajillion times," LawnStarter's Ryan Farley says, they could win the SEO game. Now, Google penalizes websites that engage in what's known as keyword stuffing.

"Nobody should be keyword stuffing anymore," Ryan says. "It won't help."

Google offers these examples of keyword stuffing:

→ Lists of phone numbers that add little value

→ Blocks of text listing cities and states that a webpage is trying to rank for

→ Repeating the same words or phrases so often that it sounds unnatural, as in this example: *We sell custom cigar humidors. Our custom cigar humidors are handmade. If you're thinking of buying a custom cigar humidor, please contact our custom cigar humidor specialists at custom.cigar.humidors@example.com.*[78]

To put it bluntly, keywording stuff can destroy your SEO strategy. *Do. Not. Ever. Do. It.* While there's no magic number, HubSpot suggests sticking to a keyword density—the percentage of times a keyword is used in copy—of 1–2 percent.[79] Keyword density beyond 2 percent, which is what happened with the meat-dress mess, could land you in Google jail.

Being Picky About Picking Your Keywords

Selecting keywords isn't a set-it-and-forget-it proposition. You can't simply settle on "meat dress" and "Lady Gaga" as keywords and move on. The process is ever evolving.

Before you choose keywords, though, you must fully understand the brand. Haley Collins recommends posing these questions to help get you to that point:

→ What does the brand sell or do?

→ How does the brand talk about itself?

→ How do customers talk about the brand?

→ What words do people use to search for information related to the brand?

"It doesn't matter if a company sells pillows but prefers to call them 'head clouds.' People who want to buy pillows are not searching online for 'head clouds,'" Haley says. "Write all you want about 'head clouds,' but don't count on selling any pillows through organic search. Google doesn't care how poetic you are."

Once you've gotten your head out of the SEO cloud, list all of the keywords that are relevant to the brand.

Next, wrap your head around the brand's marketing priorities for the period for which you'll be creating content, Haley says. What keywords would help land the brand on the first page of Google search results? For example, does the brand—let's call it Pillow People—want to focus on pillows in the first quarter of the year and sheets in the second quarter? If the first-quarter target is "pillows," narrow the list of keywords to garner traffic related to pillows, Haley suggests.

Then, she says, plug the keywords into a research tool like Moz or Semrush. Use the "questions" and "related keyphrase" filters to find the average monthly volume for keywords, including ones you may not have known about. Look for keywords with a volume that matches the type of content you're creating for Pillow People and that matches the brand's domain authority. Domain authority refers to a Moz score that predicts how likely a site is to rank in terms of search engine results. The top domain authority score is 100.[80]

In addition, type the keywords into Google.

Would those keywords benefit Pillow People? If not, try other keywords.

Are the sites showing up in search results more respected than Pillow People's site is? If so, tweak the keywords.

So, rather than going after "Why can't I sleep?"—a phrase for which Google would favor medical websites—look at "the perfect bedtime routine," which would allow a non-medical website like Pillow People's site to appear higher in search results.

For Pillow People, it makes sense to feature a page that addresses the types, colors, sizes, and shapes of pillows available on its website.

"Your various blog pieces could get into the nitty-gritty of pillows and cover everything related to pillows and their use," Haley says. "You could write about the history of pillows, getting better sleep, how pillowcase color influences sleep quality, setting a bedtime routine, the best posture for watching TV in bed, and so on—whatever life situation or search could potentially lead to the awareness or purchase of a new pillow."

Keep in mind that some online searches are what Haley calls "exploratory." They're not looking for a specific thing but, instead, a general concept. "Pillows" qualifies as an exploratory keyword. Meanwhile, if someone types "where to buy cheap throw pillows" into a search engine, it's pretty likely that they're shopping for new throw pillows.

"Picking the right keywords is a balancing act of knowing the brand and type of content you're creating," Haley says, "and then matching those elements up with keyword volume and intent."

"One of the biggest mistakes I see new SEO content writers and planners make is targeting phrases that are too big for their client's britches," she adds. "All they see is a high average monthly volume, but they don't take into account the site strength or how the client would stack up against other page one competitors. It's better to be on page one for a term with an average search volume of 20 than on page 10 for a term with an average volume of 3,500."

However you incorporate keywords into content, keep in mind that poorly written content (the meat-dress example haunts me) will repel readers in the same way that a defensive skunk sprays a nasty chemical mix to repel people and animals. Remember that you're writing primarily for the reader, not the search engines, and readers want to find answers to their questions, learn something new, or be entertained.

No one wants to consume rotten content about Lady Gaga's meat dress—or, I would venture to guess, consume the meat dress itself.

Therefore, SEO is part art, part science. The key is to deftly incorporate keywords into your SEO strategy without clobbering someone over the head with those keywords. If you lack in-depth expertise, as I do, don't wing it when it comes to SEO. Either read up on the subject, hire SEO specialists, or tap freelance SEO talent. Your brand and your audience will be better off for it.

STRIPPING IT DOWN

1. **Be patient with SEO.** Developing a well-oiled SEO strategy takes time. Yet, the time you spend on SEO can pay off handsomely in the long run.

2. **Anyone can learn SEO.** You can pick up enough SEO knowledge to succeed in content marketing without mastering the subject.

3. **Create valuable content.** Your audience will appreciate it. And so will the SEO gods like Google.

4. **Key in on keywords.** SEO keywords should be incorporated into content. But keywords shouldn't entirely drive the content.

5. **Avoid keyword "stuffing."** Overuse of keywords can put a dagger in your content marketing strategy.

four

ESTABLISHING AN EARTHQUAKE-RESILIENT FOUNDATION FOR CONTENT MARKETING SUCCESS

WHEN I WAS a newspaper reporter in the 1990s, I flew to Washington, D.C., to cover a congressional hearing. While there, I soaked up the sight of the some of the world's most iconic structures that feature pillars—the White House, the U.S. Capitol, the U.S. Supreme Court, the Jefferson Memorial. Simply awe-inspiring, particularly for a history geek and architecture admirer like me.

Most awe-inspiring, though, is the Lincoln Memorial—not only for its pillars, but for what the structure stands for. Each of the Lincoln Memorial's 36 pillars represents each of the 36 states in the Union at the time of President Abraham Lincoln's death.

Pillars adorn famous places like the Parthenon in Athens,

Greece, and the Colosseum in Rome. While pillars add a design element to a building, they more importantly bear weight or provide stability.

Pillars also add tremendous stability in content marketing. Digital marketing agency Single Grain describes pillar content as offering "a complete answer to any question a user may be searching for on a given topic. It's specifically designed to provide value for the reader, and also to rank highly in the search engines."[81]

As it relates to content, pillars support a brand's content marketing strategy. I've always referred to this type of content as "foundational" content; it's also known as cornerstone or flagship content.[82] Whatever you call it, this content "can help your site easily rank high in the search engines, gain traction and attract a tsunami of consistent traffic," according to the Serve No Master website for entrepreneurs.[83]

As outlined by Single Grain, pillar content characteristically:

→ Solves a problem or answers a question with comprehensive, accurate information. For instance, a piece of pillar content may address the question, "What is debt consolidation?"

→ Differs in scope or detail from other content on the subject. A piece of pillar content about debt consolidation may separate itself from similar content if, for example, it includes an extensive list of nonprofit debt consolidation programs.

→ Stands out as some combination of trustworthy, useful, or interesting. A piece of content about debt consolidation could be both useful and interesting if it includes an interactive element that features a debt consolidation calculator.[84]

Suffice it to say that without pillar content, your website and your content marketing strategy may crumble like the ancient Great Wall of China or Egypt's ancient Pyramids of Giza.

One piece of pillar content that fits the quality description is a roughly 3,000-word article I wrote in 2019 titled, "Everything You Need to Know About How to Start a Self-Storage Business."[85] That article appears on the website of Storable, which operates the SpareFoot self-storage marketplace. In a 2021 Google search for "how to start a self-storage business," this article appeared first in the search results.

Pillar content was a foundation of content marketing strategies I led at SpareFoot, as well as at a group of insurance websites (Bankrate Insurance) and an outdoor services platform (LawnStarter). And if you're involved in guiding the content marketing strategy of your organization, pillar content must become part of your vocabulary, just as pillars are part of the vocabulary of architects and builders.

The Pillars of Pillar Content

Haley Collins is one of my pillars when it comes to learning the ins and outs of pillar content.

While I've created pillar content myself, I've never done it with the kind of precision she does as director of operations at content marketing agency GPO. I write pillar and non-pillar content for several GPO clients. For instance, I might write a piece of pillar content titled, "The Six Most Important Maintenance Services for Your Car," while I might create a piece of related, but non-pillar, content titled, "The Six Things You Need to Know About Tire Maintenance." Think of it this way: Pillar content is broad, and non-pillar content is granular.

When Haley is tasked with producing pillar content for a client, she studies its primary products and services and then arranges pillar content by level of importance. If a GPO client sells auto insurance, you can't plunge headfirst into "What happens if my car gets totaled in an accident?" (non-pillar content) if you haven't already explained comprehensive and collision coverage and, before that, the overarching concept of auto insurance (pillar content).

"One of the key goals with pillar content and its supporting pieces is to show Google the logic, strength, and breadth of coverage and understanding within your site. You link each of these pieces together to build a stronger net and wider relationship," Haley says.

While content marketers traditionally think of pillar content as blog posts or articles, it also can come in the form of infographics, videos, and other content.[86] When trying to settle on the type of pillar content to publish, remember your audience and how they like to absorb information.

One of my favorite digital marketing authorities is Neil Patel. And, as you would expect, one of the pillar pages on his website (neilpatel.com) is a prime example of how pillar content should be done.

In his "Growth Hacking Made Simple: A Step-by-Step Guide," Patel delivers information in short sentences and paragraphs, and generously sprinkles the information with charts, graphics, and other visuals.[87] On top of that, he hyperlinks to each section of the guide, enabling you to skip what you don't want to read and zero in on what you do want to read. Also, Patel makes smart use of links to his own site (internal links) and links to other websites (outbound links). The internal links connect to a number of pieces of related content, such as "Product Life Cycle: What It Is, the 5 Stages, & Examples."

Just as Patel did, you can create a pillar page by picking the main topic, selecting the subtopics, conducting keyword research, and moving on to creating and publishing the content. You need not be a marketing wiz like Patel to produce high-quality pillar content. You must, however, put in the time and effort to generate content that's worthy of your audience and Google.

Content Clusters

LawnStarter takes a slightly different approach to pillar content. The company groups its pillar content and supporting articles into "content clusters." A cluster builds authority on a topic, with the goal of pillar content and supporting content all rising together in Google rankings. Aside from the ranking benefits, LawnStarter finds it easier to link related pieces of content at the outset when they're published all at once, as a cluster, rather than over a period of time.

Under this model, content focuses on topics rather than keywords, according to the Content Marketing Institute.

"Instead of creating one master guide that hits several keywords, a topic cluster model is an intent-based approach. It simplifies blog archives by featuring content around one central topic—referred to as the pillar page or post," the Content Marketing Institute explains. "Several supporting blog posts (or clusters) are planned, written, and published from this pillar post. These cluster posts explain subtopics based on the pillar topic and generate internal links to the pillar page."[88]

Building Your Own Lincoln Memorial of Pillar Content

A piece of pillar content probably won't feature as many pillars as the Lincoln Memorial does (36) or take as long to build (eight years), but you can envision construction of this grand structure as you assemble your strategy for pillar content. After all, architect Henry Bacon put together a detailed plan for the memorial, including how to incorporate various pieces of granite, limestone, and marble into this epic monument of the 16th president of the United States.

When you're building pillar content, you typically focus on broad, high-volume keywords for general categories or pillar pieces, Haley says. You might look at those keywords as the granite, limestone, and marble used to construct the Lincoln Memorial. More complex keywords, known as long-tail keywords, are reserved for blogs or product pages.

For clients who are building a blog from the ground up, Haley suggests a staggered approach of one piece of pillar content per month and four pieces of content per month that support the pillar content. The pillar content covers topics that will be linked forever to the blog. In other words, it's meant to be evergreen. An example of those tiers might be:

→ "How to Get Cheap Car Insurance" (pillar content)

→ "How Much Car Insurance Do I Need?" (supporting content)

→ "How to Get Car Insurance Discounts" (supporting content)

→ "Should You Raise Your Car Insurance Deductible to Save Money?" (supporting content)

→ "How Does My Driving Record Affect My Car Insurance Costs?" (supporting content)

A piece of evergreen content generally should be at least 1,000 words. GPO shoots for at least 1,200 words and up to 2,500 words for a piece of pillar content. (A 2020 survey showed the average piece of pillar content ranges from 1,000 to 4,000 words.)[89]

Evergreen content can include how-to guides, frequently asked questions (FAQs), and glossaries.[90] An example of those elements is a how-to guide I wrote for personal finance website Credit Karma. The guide dives into money issues faced by newlyweds and how to overcome such concerns. It blends straightforward advice with insights from financial experts.

Key points in the guide are:

→ Having the "money talk"

→ Establishing goals

→ Setting a budget

→ Hammering out banking details

→ Evaluating credit cards and debt

→ Discussing life insurance

→ Assessing the tax situation

→ Looking toward retirement[91]

Coming up with those bullet points involved a combination of factors: direction from Credit Karma, including suggested keywords; online research to discover common questions people ask about newlyweds and their finances; and exploration of existing content on the subject to assess how this piece of content could be better than what already appears online.

"Pillar content explains the who, what, where, when, and how of a topic, and typically covers the most commonly asked questions about a subject. Good pillar content is inherently long. It has to cover a lot of ground," GPO's Haley Collins says. "Once you publish a pillar piece, you'll naturally find yourself linking back to it and thinking, 'Oh! My reader would find this helpful!'"

GPO structures pillar content with headers, subheads, and bulleted lists—anything to help the reader grasp the purpose of each section and easily navigate the content. Haley says pillar content can be consumed from top to bottom, or it can be nibbled in bite-size chunks. The structure of the pillar content must support that aspect.

A budgeting guide I wrote for Credit Karma fits Haley's guidelines. The table of contents comprises five recommendations:

→   Set your goals.

→   Figure out where your finances stand.

→   Create a monthly budget (or whatever time frame makes sense for you).

→   Stick to the plan.

→   Review the plan.

The Credit Karma guide then delves, section by section, into each of the five recommendations. The way the guide is structured enables the reader to pick one topic to review, skim through all the topics, or spend the estimated eight minutes it takes to pore over the entire guide.[92]

Supporting content, meanwhile, hovers around 500 to 800 words (at least at Haley's company); it digs into a subject related to the pillar content.

"For example, we might do a pillar piece about 'How brakes work' and support it with five shorter blogs about brake noises, brake smells, types of brake pads, and common brake problems—all of which link back to the pillar piece and the client's main website," Haley explains.

As content is published, GPO continually returns to older posts and links them to newer ones, weaving the blog posts together and showing search engines how various topics are related.

So, when it comes to pillar content and related content, it's critical to not only build the content but maintain and nurture it. Furthermore, it's vital to mesh related pieces of content, just as it's vital to mesh the various iconic structures in Washington, D.C., as part of one grand vision.

The Credit Karma budgeting guide links to numerous pieces of supporting content, such as:

→ The best money apps for saving and investing

→ How to get out of credit card debt

→ Three steps to build a solid financial foundation

It's worth noting that each of those three pieces of supporting content is longer than the 500 to 800 words prescribed by GPO's Haley Collins. And that's okay. The three Credit Karma articles still effectively support the main guide on budgeting.

Just as with the creation of the Lincoln Memorial, your strategy for pillar content goes beyond the initial design and construction. You must constantly maintain and update the content (and the supporting content) to help prevent your pillar content from crumbling.

If, for example, you published a piece of pillar content about business credit cards in 2018, it should be tweaked or overhauled. You'll need to update the statistics, the titles of people quoted, and other pertinent information.

Be an Architect: Developing a Blueprint for Your Pillar Content

Henry Bacon spent close to 10 years working on the Lincoln Memorial, including extensive planning after the federal government hired him for the project. To be sure, creation of pillar content lacks that level of devotion. But it does take careful planning, including substantive keyword research. It also takes a big dose of devotion, as pillar content always must be tweaked and updated.

Your in-depth keyword research will help you create the proper amount of pillar content.

How much is the correct amount of pillar content? Poll results released in 2020 by Databox, a producer of dashboard software, found that among the content marketers who were questioned, nearly 45 percent indicated their website had five or fewer pillar pages.[93]

In my book, that's not enough pillar content to get the job done.

Think of how much money a business is leaving on the table by publishing so little pillar content. However, even just one piece of pillar content can yield dividends. Databox cites one company, API-integration platform Cloud Elements, that saw a 53 percent lift in organic traffic three weeks after putting out "The Definitive Guide to API Integration."[94] That's impressive.

Wouldn't we all love a 53 percent lift in organic traffic in just three weeks? You bet! Fortunately, it's quite possible for your brand to accomplish a similar feat. Setting a strong foundation for pillar content and related content—and regularly shoring up that foundation—can help you achieve the sort of results that Cloud Elements achieved.

STRIPPING IT DOWN

1. **Pay attention to pillar content.** Pillar content can, and should, be the foundation of your content marketing efforts.

2. **Support the pillars.** Be sure to complement your pillar content with offshoot content that relates to the subject of the pillar content.

3. **Consider the structure of your pillars.** Oftentimes, pillar content contains headers, subheads, and bulleted lists. Such a format makes inherently lengthy pillar contact easier to digest.

4. **Revisit your pillar content.** From time to time, pillar content should be refreshed to update data, titles of people quoted, and other information.

5. **Don't skimp on pillar content.** A couple of pieces of pillar content won't cut it. Build out a robust collection of pillars.

five

THE BADASS VALUE OF BLOGGING

BACK IN 2010, I applied for an editing job at the University of Texas McCombs School of Business. I was unemployed at the time, and that opening was by far the most attractive career opportunity I had come across. So, I submitted my application and set about asking some of my professional contacts to endorse me for the job. I asked too many of those contacts to reach out, though; the hiring manager politely but firmly told me to back off.

Despite the annoying barrage of testimonials given on my behalf, I scored an interview. Turns out I was one of four finalists for the position out of roughly 300 applicants. Alas, I didn't get the job. Upon learning that news, I pressed the hiring manager about why I wasn't chosen. He reluctantly offered two reasons: The winning candidate gelled better with the team, and the winning candidate had blogging experience (which I lacked).

Well, there wasn't a lot I could do about the first factor. But I realized that I needed to bulk up my résumé when it came to blogging. Otherwise, I figured, other employers might pass me by.

I soon launched a blog anchored in my eight years as a business journalist. The new blog, called AustInnovation, focused on tech companies in Austin and their hiring plans and practices.[95] The blog soon gained a following, attracting about 3,000 monthly pageviews roughly three months after its launch.

Fast forward a few months. I applied for an editing position in Austin at Bankrate, a provider of personal finance information. This time, I could tout my blogging credentials. And this time, I got the job. My AustInnovation blog contributed to Bankrate's decision to hire me. More importantly, it set me up for success in my first role in the field of content marketing.

For me and for organizations of all sizes, blogging is a game changer.

Survey data published in 2022 by Semrush shows blog posts rank among the most successful forms of content. Thirty-six percent of the more than 1,500 businesses questioned by Semrush indicated blogging was the form of content that brought them the best content marketing results in 2021. Blogging was preceded only by video (37 percent).[96]

"Blogging is an important part of any content marketing strategy because it is the part of your site that you will most frequently update with new posts and information to keep readers engaged. It is often through blog content that you first entice people to your site and start to build your brand's audience," according to BrightEdge, which offers an SEO platform for brands.[97]

While a content marketing strategy conceivably can thrive without blog posts, any content marketing strategy can be far more robust with blogging as a component. Blogging should be *the* cornerstone of a content marketing strategy. Fortunately, platforms like WordPress have made it simpler than ever to publish blog posts. (And if a non-techie like me can successfully navigate WordPress, anyone can.)

A prime example of this philosophy is the blog published by BioLite, a maker of outdoor energy gear.

As the Shopify blog points out, BioLite's blog "does an excellent job both quietly promoting its products and offering value to its readers." Ultimately, the blog—with its combination of posts, how-to guides, infographics, and videos—pushes BioLite toward achieving its goal of offsetting three million tons of greenhouse gases by 2025 through access to clean, renewable energy.[98] As of December 2021, BioLite had surpassed the 650,000-ton mark for greenhouse-gas offsets.[99]

These four statistics alone underscore the value of blogging for brands like BioLite:

→ Businesses with blogs generate 55 percent more visits to their website than businesses without blogs.[100]

→ Blogging helps you pick up as much as 97 percent more links to your website.[101]

→ Businesses with blogs attract two times more email traffic than businesses without blogs.[102]

→ A whopping 61 percent of consumers have made a purchase based on a blog post.[103]

Even just one blog post can supercharge a website.

In 2019, the GrowthBadger website enjoyed an 843 percent spike in traffic in one week based on a single blog post. For the post, GrowthBadger's Kyle Byers surveyed more than 1,100 bloggers about their strategies and shared the results in a blog post.[104]

Not only was the post shared more than 1,000 times in that first week, but it attracted backlinks from 109 websites. Those social shares and backlinks, mostly from more authoritative websites, singlehandedly pushed up GrowthBadger's domain authority.[105]

Now, I wouldn't suggest a one-and-done approach—publishing a single blog post, praying it performs magic, and then slacking off on the rest of your blogging strategy. To sustain and grow traffic to your website, you must steadily publish blog posts.

Why Is Blog Content as Vital as Water?

In many cases, blog content represents someone's first engagement with your brand.

For instance, if your company provides lawn care services (as my former employer LawnStarter does), a blog post about caring for your lawn in the summer directly targets the type of potential customer you're trying to attract. A visitor to your site is often hunting for an answer to a question. When a blog post on your site answers a commonly asked question, then you're addressing a need.

In content marketing, it's vital to blog about topics that people are Googling, rather than topics you feel like opining about. Chances are, no one landing on your lawn care blog cares what you have to say about the best video games.

Finding out which topics are on people's minds can start by simply plugging a few words into a Google search query. For example, when I was working at LawnStarter, I was curious which U.S. metro areas employed the most lawn care workers. I did a Google search (using something like "areas that employ the most lawn care workers") and learned the U.S. Bureau of Labor Statistics published data about the number of front-line lawn care workers employed in metro areas across the country. I combed through the data and discovered the Palm Coast metro area of Florida boasted the most lawn care workers per capita.[106]

If a consumer views your lawn care content as helpful and credible, it might spur them to put their lawn care in your hands. Even if that doesn't happen, blog posts that zero in on your company's area of expertise boost your authority in that area. And if Google's algorithms view the blog post as a piece of top-notch, well-crafted, in-depth content, then Google will push it higher in search rankings than a piece of crappy content.

Avoiding the Trap of Crappy Content

To test this theory, I searched in 2021 for the phrase "how to start a self-storage business" on Google. What popped up first in the search was a comprehensive post I wrote in 2019 for SpareFoot about how to start a self-storage business.

The roughly 3,000-word post sought to inform readers about how to start a self-storage business. To do so, I broke down the story into various chunks:

→ How much will it cost to start a self-storage business?

→ What kind of research and planning do you need to do before starting a self-storage business?

→ Should you buy an existing self-storage facility?

→ Should you build a self-storage facility from the ground up?

→ How will you manage and market your self-storage facility?[107]

I created it as pillar content. All of those questions on their own can be (and should be) answered in separate blog posts. But in developing a well-rounded blog post about how to start a self-storage business, it was essential to tackle those questions.

Keep in mind that many folks won't read an entire blog post about how to start a self-storage business. Most likely, they'll dive into the parts of the post that they want to consume and either skim or ignore the rest. But at least you've given readers a lot of content to choose from. In the mind of a reader, a blog post of such caliber can assert a brand's authority.

Getting Your Blogging Strategy on Track

Before you start randomly publishing blog posts, you must figure out the purpose of your blog and your audience.

When I was steering the content marketing strategy at SpareFoot, we zeroed in on two blogging tracks: B2C and B2B.

For the B2C blog, we focused, of course, on the basics of self-storage and moving (which prompts a lot of self-storage rentals). But we also went all in on organizing as a key topic because organizing also drives a fair number of self-storage rentals. We sought to be a go-to source for organizing tips and tricks. That focus produced blog posts like "17 New Year's Resolutions to Help You Get Organized"[108] and "Before and After: 4 Great Decluttering Success Stories."[109]

The B2B blogs, on the other hand, catered to folks in the self-storage industry, such as facility owners and real estate brokers.

We concentrated on covering the industry as if SpareFoot were a news outlet in hopes of delivering information that industry insiders couldn't find anywhere else. After all, the self-storage sector is a nearly $40 billion industry in the U.S.[110] that attracts little attention from mainstream media. Among the blog posts that have been published in that regard are "Self-storage industry reacts to the coronavirus pandemic"[111] and "California storage owners face potentially 'disastrous' tax hike."[112]

Once you've nailed down a blog's purpose and audience, it's time to settle on how often you should publish content.

At SpareFoot and LawnStarter, we published several posts a week. However, it's not mandatory to crank out that many posts. In fact, there's no perfect number for how often to publish blog posts.

But the more often you publish blog posts, the more traffic you're inclined to pick up.

Data cited by HubSpot indicates that companies publishing at least 15 blog posts a month attract five times more traffic than companies that publish no blog posts. And it's not just corporate behemoths that benefit from such frequency. According to HubSpot, small businesses (those with up to 10 employees) tend to witness the biggest gains in web traffic when they publish more blog posts.[113]

However often you decide to publish blog posts, be consistent. If you pick a three-times-a-week schedule, stick to it. Readers want to know that they can depend on a regular cadence of content from a favorite blog. When you adopt a haphazard approach to publishing, you lose that cadence—and potentially lose your audience. Perhaps even more importantly, Google respects a regular influx of fresh content. The more often you publish, the more Google will crawl your website for fresh content.

But don't pump out content for the sake of pumping out content. Emphasize quality over quantity when it comes to blog posts or any other content you create. If that means publishing just one blog post every Tuesday, then do it. Know what your capability is in order to consistently meet your objective.

Every blog post and other piece of content should be approached journalistically, meaning that trusted sources of information should be cited and data should be double-checked. In other words, don't pull every shred of data from Wikipedia. Yes, Wikipedia is convenient. No, it's not reliable.

So, once you've crafted a blogging strategy, how do you keep track of all the moving parts?

Well, you could use something as simple as a spreadsheet to plot your blog posts and other content. In a spreadsheet, you'd want to include basics like the title, content creator, due date, and publication date.

You also might consider investing in software to map out your content calendar. My favorite software in this category is the easy-to-use Trello platform, but others worth checking out include CoSchedule, HubSpot, and WordPress Editorial Calendar. If possible, sign up for free trials of editorial calendar software to find the product that best suits your needs.

What Can You Do Aside from Blogging?

While I'm a huge fan of blogging—I'm a writer, after all—I realize it's not the only content marketing tool that can or should be in your content marketing toolkit. Whereas a blog post may not generate as much traffic as you'd hoped for, a different kind of content might deliver amazing results.

For instance, an infographic I created in 2013 in conjunction with a marketing company called NowSourcing got picked up by the Mashable website—a huge win for Bankrate Insurance, where I was leading content marketing strategy at the time. In an attractive, easy-to-digest format, the infographic conveyed a carload of data about self-driving cars.[114] I doubt that a blog post containing the same data would have gotten the attention of Mashable or any other high-profile website.

Aside from infographics, other non-blog content you might fold into your content marketing strategy includes:

→ **E-books.** Here's an astonishing statistic: The global e-book market was valued at $18.1 billion in 2020 and is expected to reach $23.1 billion by 2026, according to Mordor Intelligence. While a $5 billion increase might not seem massive, remember we're talking billions!

Regardless, the popularity of e-books is rising.[115]

→ **Instagram posts.** About one billion people use Instagram each month, according to data published in 2021 by the Hootsuite social media platform.[116] The photo-and video-sharing app helps companies promote their brand stories to people from Alabama to Wyoming and beyond.

→ **Podcasts.** About 80 million Americans ages 12 and over listen to podcasts each week, according to data published in 2021 by Edison Research.[117]

→ **Videos.** People around the world are voracious viewers of videos. Nearly three-fourths of American adults watch videos on YouTube, according to data cited in 2021 by Hootsuite. And about 1.7 billion unique monthly visitors head to YouTube.[118] Oh, and don't overlook the short-form video app TikTok, which reported in September 2021 that it had one billion active users around the world.[119]

→ **Webinars.** The COVID-19 pandemic sparked greater interest in webinars due to lockdowns and social-distancing protocols. Data released in 2020 by the Content Marketing Institute indicates B2B marketers stepped up their use of webinars, virtual events, and online courses during the pandemic, going from 57 percent to 67 percent. Even at 57 percent, webinars and similar content shouldn't be overlooked, especially in a B2B context.[120]

In my roles as a content marketing strategist, I've concentrated mostly on blog posts and infographics. Why? Because the resources at my disposal limited me to those two kinds of content. For me, blog posts and infographics have gotten the job done. For other folks, podcasts or videos might be the primary vehicles for content marketing.

Don't be afraid to dabble in various types of content, experimenting with what works and what doesn't work. But don't feel that your content marketing strategy must feature myriad types of content. You don't want to stretch yourself too thin, thus potentially diluting the power of your content.

Become the "Answer Person"

No matter whether you lean heavily on blog posts or you offer a mix of content, the information you dispense should, first and foremost, be useful to the consumer of that content. In this regard, think of your organization as the "answer man."

From the 1960s to the 1990s, the Shell oil conglomerate aired a series of TV commercials featuring the "Shell Answer Man." As a whole, the ads sought to supply tips about car maintenance.[121] Anyone of a certain age (including myself) likely saw those TV spots on a regular basis.

While the name "Shell Answer Man" wrongly suggests that only a guy can answer questions about car maintenance, I bring up this ad campaign as an example of how a brand sought to be the go-to source of information about car maintenance. It was a genius move, considering that almost every current or potential Shell customer was (and still is) a motorist.

Each blog post you publish should, at least in part,

answer a question rattling around in the mind of a current or potential customer or constituent. Fortunately, you need not pay exorbitant amounts of money to conduct research about questions that your audience is pondering.

If you're low on human resources, financial resources, or both, you can simply plug questions into Google to get a sense for content online that addresses those questions. Don't dismiss even the simplest of questions.

For instance, I realized when I was working for Bankrate Insurance that we needed a piece of content answering the question "What is insurance?" It's easy to assume that everyone knows the answer to that question, but making such an assumption can be a disservice to your audience.

You also might visit Google Trends. This tool analyzes the top search queries in Google. Google Trends can turn up fascinating but run-of-the mill data or even quirky insights.

Over the years, I've built entire blog posts around data I've harvested from Google Trends. One post I crafted for LawnStarter, based on Google Trends data, reported which metro areas expressed the most interest in garden gnomes. The answer: Baltimore. Why Baltimore? It turns out the Baltimore Orioles baseball team gave away Orioles-related garden gnomes at a game in 2015 and at another game in 2016.[122]

The wonderful thing about digging up data you discover on Google, in Google Trends, or in other places online is that it can serve as the foundation for rankings, lists, how-to guides, pros-and-cons reviews, and other valuable content. In other words, you can come up with a seemingly endless supply of content thanks to satisfying your intellectual curiosity about what your audience has on their minds.

The internet can be a minefield, but it also can be fertile territory for blog posts and other material capable of driving traffic and driving interest in your brand.

In the end, it's dangerous to write off the value of blogging. Blogging can form the foundation of your content marketing initiatives, and can supply a ready route for readers to repeatedly and enthusiastically engage with your brand. Even if your brand publishes only a couple of blog posts per week, those posts can be the jumping-off point for the development and success of your content marketing efforts.

STRIPPING IT DOWN

1. **Emphasize blogging.** Blogging should be the cornerstone of your content marketing strategy. Blog posts remain among the most popular forms of content in the content marketing universe.

2. **Stay in your lane.** Don't veer off into blog posts not related to your brand. A toy brand probably shouldn't be blogging about lingerie, for instance.

3. **Know your audience.** Pinpoint what kind of content resonates most with your blog readers. Make sure you always deliver that kind of content.

4. **Be consistent.** Publish blog posts on a regular schedule. Your audience will come to expect a cadence to your blogging.

5. **Complement your blogging.** Consider publishing content like infographics, e-books, and Instagram posts to supplement your blog posts.

six

EVERY ORGANIZATION IS A STORYTELLER

IN A CONFERENCE room at Children's Hospital Colorado in the Denver suburb of Aurora, I saw one of the best pieces of content I've ever consumed. It had such an impact on me that I remember it to this day.

In 2013, I was among the attendees of a content marketing conference sponsored by Chicago-based Ragan Communications, one of the best resources available for information and insights about content marketing. During one of the conference sessions, we heard a presentation by a representative of a nonprofit called charity: water.[123] The highlight of the presentation turned out to be a video produced by charity: water.

The video, shot in Ethiopia, tells the story of Rachel Beckwith. For her ninth birthday in 2011, Rachel requested $300 in donations for charity: water to supply clean water to 15 people. She fell $80 shy of her goal. Sadly, Rachel died just a month after turning nine years old from injuries suffered in a car crash. Following Rachel's death, her birthday wish circulated around the world, resulting in donations exceeding $1.2 million to charity: water.[124]

In 2012, on the first day of her job as a videographer for charity: water, Jamie Pent flew to Ethiopia to capture the visit by Rachel's mother, Samantha, and Rachel's grandparents to the village that benefited from Rachel's birthday fundraiser. Ragan says the charity: water story could have been told through a blog post, slideshow, or Facebook page, but Pent believed "video forges stronger connections." The result: a nearly five-minute video that beautifully chronicled the trip, which coincided with the one-year anniversary of Rachel's death.[125]

When I initially watched the video, I welled up with tears. The same thing happened when I watched the video again just recently. Whether you're a crier or not, I challenge anyone to be emotionally unaffected by this video.

In no small part, I attribute the power of the video to Pent's masterful storytelling, shooting, and editing skills. For me, perhaps the most touching aspect of the video was seeing the constant, enormous smile on the face of Samantha Beckwith, Rachel's mother, as she pumped water from a well and visited with the Ethiopian villagers who now enjoyed access to clean water. To know that so much good had been done by Rachel's campaign should put a smile on anyone's face.

Telling Your Story

Of course, not every organization will be able to tell a story as uplifting as the one told in Pent's video. But that doesn't mean your organization can't tell impactful stories. They could come in the form of videos uploaded to YouTube or posts on Instagram or Q&As published on your blog. And they need not be as artfully crafted as Pent's charity: water video.

What matters most is that you convey a compelling story. Maybe the story focuses on one of your organization's clients who has achieved success by using your products or services. Or perhaps it shines a spotlight on a team of staffers who developed a solution to address slow responses to inbound phone calls.

As you contemplate how to tell your organization's story, consider what makes your organization special. Which emotions can you tap into?

→ Is it the amazing corporate culture?

→ Is it the one-of-a-kind product or service that you offer?

→ Is it the entrepreneurial spirit behind your organization's success?

What about your organization will attract people to your content?

At SpareFoot, one of the stories we were able to tell centered on co-founders Chuck Gordon and Mario Feghali. In 2008, Gordon was enrolled at UCLA and about to take off on a study abroad trip to Singapore. But he needed to find a place to stash his stuff while he was away.[126] He found the process of locating a storage space to be tedious.

Gordon and Feghali, a fellow UCLA student, then hatched the idea for SpareFoot. It began as a peer-to-peer storage platform. But based on input from self-storage operators eager to find a way to market their space, Gordon and Feghali soon pivoted to a platform for consumers to rent storage units. Today, SpareFoot ranks as the world's largest online marketplace for self-storage.[127]

While Gordon, CEO of Storable, concedes that "there's nothing less sexy than storage space,"[128] SpareFoot and the broader Storable organization have something of a sexy story to tell. Who doesn't like to learn about innovative entrepreneurs and successful businesses?

Plus, most of us like to read or hear tales about our collective "junk," which self-storage units often house for months on end. "People always need some place to store their junk," Alice Chung, a commercial real estate analyst at Moody's Investors Service, observed in 2018.[129]

Another less-than-sexy industry is lawn care. Co-founded by Steven Corcoran, Ryan Farley, and Jonas Weigert, LawnStarter operates a platform that matches consumers with providers of lawn care and other outdoor services.[130]

"Six years ago, my two college friends and I started LawnStarter, an on-demand platform for lawn service," Ryan told the *Austin Business Journal* in 2019. "At first there was just the three of us and an intern in a two-bedroom apartment with no furniture. We lived on bulk purchases from Costco knowing that what we were building would become something much bigger."[131]

Indeed, LawnStarter has gotten much bigger. In 2021, eight years after it was founded, LawnStarter purchased one of its rivals, Lawn Love.[132] The acquisition and ongoing growth enable LawnStarter to continue telling an interesting story about the blossoming of a business in a pretty uninteresting industry.

While your industry may be mundane, your organization's story need not be.

Both SpareFoot and LawnStarter tell their stories largely through the written word—namely, blog posts and press releases. When I worked at both companies, we leaned heavily on those two avenues, relying much less on video, social media, or other storytelling tools.

But what's best for SpareFoot and LawnStarter may not be best for your content marketing program. In other words, you should embrace content marketing methods that will resonate most with your intended audience, whether that's customers, investors, prospective employees, or others. If you're in charge of content marketing for a lifestyle brand, for instance, Instagram or TikTok may be the ticket to telling your brand's story. To settle on the best storytelling tools, you need to figure out who your audience is and where they consume content.

What Is Your Identity?
Learning from Oracle, Tesla, and YETI

Just as every person has an identity, every brand has an identity. For instance, a tech start-up may portray itself as upbeat, fun, and laid-back. To the contrary, a Fortune 500 company in the heavily regulated financial services sector might telegraph an image as a traditional, straight-by-the-book business.

Three publicly traded companies—Oracle, Tesla, and YETI—based here in my backyard in Austin, Texas, demonstrate just how much brand identity differs from one organization to the next. While I don't use any of Oracle's, Tesla's, or YETI's products, I do keep close track of the companies, if for no reason other than they're based in the city where I live.

On its website, Oracle explains that its mission "is to help people see data in new ways, discover insights, unlock endless possibilities."[133] The tech giant, appearing at No. 80 on the 2021 version of the Fortune 500, specializes in cloud computing and database software.[134] In 2020, *Forbes* magazine placed Oracle at No. 16 on its list of the most valuable global brands with a significant U.S. presence.[135]

As a company whose offerings include a cloud-based content marketing platform for businesses, Oracle takes content marketing quite seriously. The platform emphasizes the Five Ps of content marketing: plan, produce, publish, promote, and prove.[136] At one time, a job posting for director of content marketing at Oracle Advertising and Customer Experience, charged with overseeing the company's three blogs, offered a glimpse into how Oracle tackles its in-house Five Ps.

"As Oracle's marketing organization continues its transformation, we're going all in on a web-first strategy and our number one goal is organic traffic," the job posting said. "In this role, you'll lead a small team to build the content factory through strategic SEO programs and by setting standards for internal and external contributors."

In its own approach to content marketing, reflecting its own identity, Oracle doesn't make waves. It's a steady-as-she-goes ship. *Fortune* magazine noted in 2021 that CEO Safra Catz "has the challenging job of repositioning the database company as a titan amid fierce competition from the likes of Amazon Web Services (AWS) and Microsoft." The magazine added that "Oracle continues to cruise along in a rapidly changing industry."[137]

That assertion hardly describes Tesla, another Austin-based company.

The maker of electric vehicles isn't cruising along. It's like a speed boat racing through—and for the most part successfully navigating—rough waters. Tesla's brand identity is tied primarily to its mercurial co-founder and CEO, billionaire Elon Musk.

A 2019 report from career platform Hired cited Musk as the most inspiring leader in the tech sector,[138] with former colleagues viewing him as everything from brilliant to temperamental.[139] Words used by outsiders to characterize him include innovator, genius, and visionary.[140]

Much of the world's exposure to Tesla comes not via standard content marketing (blogs, for instance) but through Musk's Twitter account, which had roughly 54 million followers as of May 2021.[141] He's also a regular fixture on YouTube.[142]

While it's hard to assign a value to Musk's social media soapbox, *Forbes* estimated in 2018 that Musk's Twitter account alone represented a $40 million marketing platform for Tesla.[143] Since then, the value of Musk's Twitter account almost certainly has skyrocketed.

No matter where he pops up, Musk runs toward controversy, rather than away from it (as many other CEOs would do).

"Elon Musk's social media presence is so strong because he is unabashedly authentic, engaging, and fun," according to PostBeyond, which helps companies build social engagement.[144]

Musk's obsession with social media contrasts with Tesla's disdain for traditional media. Tesla disbanded its public relations department in 2020 and no longer responds to media inquiries.[145] Plus, the automaker spends next to nothing on traditional advertising.[146]

Yet, thanks mostly to the sheer force of nature that is Elon Musk, Tesla attracts a mountain of attention. The distinction demonstrates that unconventional content marketing strategies, however loosely organized they may be, can pay hefty dividends.

The third and final Austin-based company I'd like to spotlight is YETI. It makes outdoor and recreational products like coolers, drinkware, backpacks, and apparel. YETI garners high praise for the high quality of its merchandise.[147]

"We decided early on that product innovation would come from necessity and firsthand experience—not from market research and data analysis," YETI explains.[148]

YETI delivers its brand message through a "meaningful" presence on social media and a commitment to "robust" content.[149] But neither the social media content nor the rest of the content is staid. The "wild at heart" brand appeals to current and potential customers based on their shared love of the outdoors.[150] Its group of brand "ambassadors"—hunters, snowboarders, fishermen, cowboys, and other adventure seekers—help spread the word as influencers.

YETI tells its stories on Facebook, Instagram, and YouTube.[151] The lifestyle brand goes a step further by publishing a beautiful print and online magazine titled *YETI Dispatch*.[152] Think of it as the once-ubiquitous Sears catalog on steroids.

Getting to the Core of Your Core Values

Even if you are not a visionary or your brand is not on a *Forbes* list, you should keep your organization's core values in mind when you're crafting and executing a content marketing strategy.

You want your strategy to align with the brand's core values. Otherwise, your messaging could come off as disjointed.

Oracle's core value encompasses 10 tenets. Among the ones that dovetail with content marketing are communication, innovation, quality, and compliance.

On the subject of innovation, Oracle says: "We welcome new ideas and dare to try new things. Problems are solved where creativity and technical expertise meet."[153]

With a focus on creativity and technical expertise, Oracle's extensive collection of blogs covers an array of topics, including customer experience, cloud computing, marketing, analytics, corporate citizenship, and software development.[154]

Meanwhile, Tesla lacks a defined set of core values.[155] But even in the absence of core values, it's clear what Tesla *does* value.

The company's stated mission is "to accelerate the world's transition to sustainable energy."[156] In tandem with that mission, Tesla strives to drive innovation.[157] The company's somewhat casual attitude toward a concrete set of core values appears to be working: In 2021, it reigned as the world's most valuable automotive brand.[158]

Unlike Tesla, YETI does outline a set of core values. One of the values that meshes especially well with its ethos is to "be authentic and innovative with our brand and products."[159] This core value certainly breaks through in YETI's content marketing. While not specified among its core values, YETI also stresses "that time spent outdoors matters more than ever and our gear can make that time extraordinary."[160]

Through content marketing, those and other principles seep through the pores of YETI's identity. Be like YETI. Make sure your brand's principles and vision are a key strand in its brand DNA.

What Makes Your Company Stand Tall Like Shaquille O'Neal?

Unless your business differentiates itself from the competition, it risks being ignored, particularly by prospective customers. Your content marketing strategy can help underpin this differentiation, but the distinction can happen only if you grasp what makes your company stand out.

Oracle, for instance, does battle with the likes of AWS and Microsoft—no small feat. So, how does a company like Oracle go toe-to-toe with other tech titans? Through product innovation.

In 2019, for instance, Oracle rolled out an autonomous operating system to go up against offerings from AWS and Microsoft. And Oracle touts what it believes is another competitive advantage: simplifying the management of IT infrastructures.

Tesla's competitive advantages lie in innovation and quality. Its approach includes a superior lineup of batteries for electric vehicles, a massive network of charging stations, a reputation for making top-notch products, and, of course, its stratospheric brand recognition.[161]

Despite its lofty position in the automotive world, Tesla can't afford to take its foot off the pedal. General Motors, among other rivals, is gunning to grab market share from Tesla.[162] But no auto manufacturer can claim the powerful marketing weapon that Tesla can: Elon Musk.

A super-icon in the form of an individual isn't the only way to garner positive attention, however. YETI, for example, doesn't rely on an outspoken, out-front spokesperson like Musk. YETI can count on the outstanding reputation of its products and customer praise.

Gear Patrol, for instance, lauds YETI's hard-sided (and pricey) coolers for their ability to keep items cold longer than other coolers, and praises the coolers' durability, sleekness, and varied color palette.[163] More broadly, YETI "is touted as the yardstick by which other outdoor accessories like coolers, drinkware, and gear are measured."[164] That's a pretty cool compliment—and one whose essence can be woven into the fabric of YETI's content marketing initiatives.

Maybe your brand is not Oracle, Tesla, or YETI. I get it. That disparity doesn't excuse you from pinning down your brand's identity and core values, though. Determining them will help bolster your brand's content marketing strategy. Questions you might ask to identify your predominant attributes include:

- → What makes your brand stand out?

- → What are your brand's core values?

- → What is your brand's mission?

- → How do you want your brand to be perceived?

Once you come up with the answers to those questions, you'll be on the right path toward establishing your brand story and clearly telling it to your audience.

STRIPPING IT DOWN

1. **Settle on what makes your brand special.** This definition should always infuse your brand's storytelling.

2. **Determine your brand identity.** Whether your brand is traditional or wacky, your brand storytelling should mirror the organization's overall vibe.

3. **Remember your core values.** Your brand's core values should help dictate the types of stories you tell, as well as the storytelling methods.

4. **Nail down your brand's edge.** Whatever your brand's competitive advantage is should be reflected in your content.

5. **Focus on perception.** When someone consumes content from your brand, how do you want them to view the brand?

seven

THE IMPORTANCE OF BEING A WILLIAM SHAKESPEARE

ONE OF MY favorite modern-day storytellers is Steve Hartman, who brilliantly weaves stories for CBS News's folksy, charming, must-see "On the Road" segments.

"Each of his segments is a master class in telling tales that thoughtfully blend emotion, wonder, humor, and above all, heart," communication strategist Mike Plotnick observes.[165]

One of those "master class" tales was a segment that aired in September 2021. It focused on the face-to-face meeting of World War II veteran Frank Grasberger and a young woman, Dashauna Priest, who wrote a letter to the veteran when she was in third grade. In the letter, Priest thanked Grasberger for his military service. Grasberger treasured the letter. The two got together 12 years after Priest penned the letter.[166]

Hartman deftly told the story of the veteran and the former student. When I saw the story on TV, it struck me as heartfelt without being sappy, touching without being overwrought. It struck the right tone.

Hartman manages to strike the right tone with every one of his "On the Road" pieces, shining a spotlight on ordinary people and their seemingly ordinary experiences. Hartman delivers powerful "On the Road" segments week after week.

In the realm of storytelling, Hartman stands tall. Your brand can stand tall, too, by bringing well-executed stories to your audience. While most of those stories won't be Hartman-caliber stories, they still can pack a punch.

Well-crafted narratives related to your brand, product, or service add realism to your content marketing. Digital marketing strategist Sujan Patel—who, like me, lives in Austin and occupied an office one floor above where I once worked—explains that we're all consumers of good stories. Customers of your brand are no different.

"Telling your story is a critical part of your brand. It helps to shape how people view you and enables consumers to begin forging a connection with you and your company," Patel notes.

"Do it right, and you'll put building blocks in place that allow you to develop a thriving brand with an equally thriving future, one that people buy from simply because they love what you do, what you stand for, and the stories you share."[167]

Patel puts it well. Yet, graduating from knowing that your brand must share its stories to knowing how to craft those stories is no easy feat. With the proper effort, your brand's stories can sparkle. But if your effort is half-assed, your brand's stories run the risk of sputtering.

An Rx for Storytelling

An article I wrote in the fall of 2021 for the quarterly magazine published by the Texas Osteopathic Medical Association puts this reality into perspective. My editor, Crystal Zuzek, assigned a 2,000-word piece (a piece I would certainly drop in the content marketing bucket) about how three osteopathic physicians in Texas had weathered the COVID-19 pandemic. Crystal, a former colleague from the *Austin Business Journal,* emailed me a set of questions to pose to the three doctors and gave me their contact information.

When I interviewed each of the doctors by phone, it would have been easy to switch to autopilot mode and blast my way through the list of questions Crystal had supplied.

My journalism experience has taught me, however, that you can't stick to a script. You must listen to the folks you're talking to and latch onto information that might be fodder for questions you hadn't planned to ask. Such was the case during my interview with Dr. Bruce Addison, a small-town physician in West Texas.

During my more than 50-minute conversation with Dr. Addison, he informed me that his longtime nurse practitioner had died in 2020 due to COVID-19. My ears and my brain perked up almost immediately. Here's a medical professional who not only dealt with treating patients during a pandemic but dealt with the loss of a longtime colleague. The death of his nurse practitioner would add a highly personal element to a story that easily could have skimped on the human side of practicing medicine.

Once I had wrapped up all three interviews, it was clear that

I had to open the article with Dr. Addison's heart-wrenching loss of his nurse practitioner. In a draft I submitted to my editor, here's how I started the story:

Last October, Dr. Bruce Addison, DO waved goodbye to the First Flight ambulance transporting his longtime nurse practitioner to the 400-bed Shannon Medical Center in San Angelo from the 14-bed hospital in the small West Texas town of McCamey—the Wind Energy Capital of Texas. If the ambulance was traveling along U.S. Highway 67 North at normal speeds, the 120-mile trip would take about two hours.

That October day would be the last time Addison would see his nurse practitioner. The 53-year-old woman died a month later due to COVID-19.

For osteopathic physicians like Addison, the COVID-19 pandemic has been eye-opening. They've witnessed severe illness and death. They've struggled to counteract medical misinformation. They've urged patients—sometimes successfully, sometimes not—to be vaccinated against COVID-19. They've coped with a heightened level of personal stress and fear.

Those three paragraphs built the foundation for exploring how three osteopathic physicians had wrestled with personal and professional concerns during a once-in-a-lifetime healthcare crisis. The details I wove into those three paragraphs—14-bed hospital, 120-mile trip, 53-year-old woman, and so forth—helped carry the narrative forward.

So, how does that description relate to storytelling for your brand? It emphasizes the importance of telling a compelling story. I could have easily cranked out a dull article that lacked a pulse. But that depiction would have been a disservice to me, my client, and my interview subjects. Besides, I doubt that a dull article would have instilled confidence in my client to keep sending assignments my way. As a writer, I'm always open to new assignments, and delivering good content translates directly into keeping clients. But more importantly, giving each story the justice it deserves earns attention that can resonate beyond your expectations.

Regardless of how your brand tells stories, it's crucial to tell stories that engage, inform, and enlighten your audience while aligning with your brand's core values. If you don't accomplish that task, you'll drive your audience to another blog post, another video, or some other piece of content—content that one of your competitors might have produced.

Seeing the Story Through an Unfiltered Lens

To get a better handle on high-quality brand storytelling, let's take a closer look at one my favorite brands, Warby Parker.

I've been wearing prescription eyeglasses for more than four decades. That's a long time, right? So, I like to think of myself as a discerning consumer of vision products. Warby Parker's brand ethos helped draw me to them, and now I'm a loyal customer.

Warby Parker stands out as a mission-driven business. The company, for instance, has helped distribute more than eight million pairs of free eyeglasses through its "Buy a Pair, Give a Pair" initiative.[168]

"Our customers, employees, community and environment are our stakeholders. We consider them in every decision that we make," Warby Parker proclaims on its website.[169]

Furthermore, as Sujan Patel points out, Warby Parker takes

consumers behind the scenes of how its glasses are made.[170]

Most notably, all Warby Parker frames are hand-assembled and polished. Gorgeous photos and marvelous videos pull back the curtain on the Warby Parker manufacturing process, showing how logos are applied, hinges are tested, and so on.[171] The company smartly devotes an entire "How Warby Parker glasses are made" section to this subject on its website.

To me, a consummate eyecare consumer, the Warby Parker story conveys how much it cares about its customers, its products, and the entire world. It's clear from its storytelling that Warby Parker understands and appreciates its customer base. Every company should hope to be worthy of telling such an eye-opening story. (Yes, I went there with a vision pun.)

"Brand storytelling is the cohesive narrative that weaves together the facts and emotions that your brand evokes. In addition to giving your customers reasons why they should buy a product or service, businesses need to start sharing the story behind their brand, why it exists, and why this matters, consistently across all communication," *Forbes* contributor Celinne Da Costa noted in 2019.[172]

To ensure you're on the right track with your brand's storytelling, be sure you've got a firm grip on what the brand does, who its audience is, and what you want people to know about your brand. Such definition might be as simple as researching your brand the way a competitor might or merely asking loads of questions internally.

Being Your Own Steve Hartman

Sure, it's relatively simple for a major brand like Warby Parker to excel at brand storytelling. They've got deep pockets and almost limitless resources. But that advantage doesn't mean your brand can't engage in stellar storytelling.

So, how do you make it all happen? Well, you can start by learning more about brand storytelling. It turns out that a variety of brand-storytelling courses are out there, and a lot of them are free or fairly inexpensive. Providers of such courses include HubSpot Academy,[173] Coursera,[174] Udemy,[175] Northwestern University,[176] and the University of Texas at Austin.[177]

Once you get up to speed on brand storytelling, you must figure out what your brand's story is. To get a better sense of your brand's story, interview people inside your organization (not just high-level executives), and ask what's at the heart of the brand:

→   What prompted the founding of the brand?

→   What is the organization's mission?

→   What motivates folks inside the organization to keep showing up for work?

→   How would you describe the culture?

→   How do you want insiders and outsiders to perceive the brand?

Answers to those and other questions can help shape the brand's storytelling.

Aside from digging into the core of the brand, you should

determine who your audience is. Obviously, your primary audience is your brand's clientele. But who are they? What are their demographics, such as age, gender, and geographic location? What do they like (and dislike) about your brand? What makes them tick? What's motivating them to seek out your brand's goods or services?

That information will be instrumental in developing your brand's persona and in accurately telling your brand's story.

The 99designs website explains that a brand's persona "is a literal depiction of a brand as a person, giving a face to the abstract characteristics, values, and voice that businesses cultivate. It involves constructing an imaginary person, complete with a fictitious name, hobbies, likes and dislikes—much like how a writer might create a character profile."[178]

For Warby Parker, the character profile centers on a 25- to 44-year-old eyecare consumer who values a brand's social impact (the company donates millions of eyeglasses and follows eco-friendly practices), eagerly welcomes e-commerce, and comfortably navigates the mobile web.

Keep in mind that consumers of your brand's stories might fall outside the typical definition of a brand persona. For example, you probably want your brand's storytelling to resonate with current and future employees. And if you work at a start-up, you likely want your brand's storytelling to appeal to potential investors. But first and foremost, your brand's storytelling should be squarely aimed at your primary customers.

Crafting the Brand Story

"Storytelling is the most powerful way to put ideas into the world."

— Author, lecturer, and consultant Robert McKee[179]

Equipped with newfound insights about brand storytelling and about your brand, you can now head down the storytelling path. If you approach storytelling the right way, that path can be smooth and rewarding.

So, what's the correct approach to brand storytelling? What might be best for one brand might not be so great for another brand, but in general you should follow these four principles.

1. **Don't get overly complicated.**

    Your brand might deal with complex subjects, but your stories need not come off as material for a physics textbook. You certainly don't want to talk above your audience. You also don't want to talk down to them, either. That approach is a tough balance to strike. However, it's vital to do so if you hope to keep your audience engaged. Keep things simple but not simplistic.

2. **Be authentic.**

    Nobody gravitates toward brands that are phony. Therefore, authenticity should be a key driver of your brand's storytelling.

    Honesty should be a constant thread throughout your messaging. If current and future consumers of your brand get the sense that your brand isn't genuine, then it won't take long for them to run off to one of your competitors.

3. **Ease up on the particulars about process.**

For some brands, it's easy to get caught up in the gee-whiz aspects of products and services. Don't get me wrong: It makes perfect sense to share details like the types of software that propel your products or services. However, that sort of information should be put in the right context.

What's more important than how your brand's gizmos and gadgets work is how they benefit your customers. No one really cares how the sausage is made; we just want to savor the flavor.

4. **Emphasize the human element.**

Your brand's stories should be character driven.

If you're telling a story about your brand's new widget, then why not tell that story through the eyes of a customer who's taking advantage of the new widget?

Or perhaps someone within your company invented the widget to help solve the global shortage of clean drinking water. Maybe a story about this inside-the-company innovator would be in order.

Of course, if your brand is all about animals, then you'll want to shift the narrative to those creatures (along with the people associated with them).

Communicating the Brand Story
Like Oprah Winfrey Would

Once you've decided how to shape your brand's storytelling, you must settle on how to convey your brand's stories. Fortunately, you've got a number of storytelling tools at your disposal these days: blogs, videos, white papers, case studies, infographics, and social media posts, to name a few.

Also keep in mind that we don't obtain information from just one source. In 2021, U.S. adults spent an astonishing average of 13 hours and 21 minutes per day consuming a variety of media in both digital and traditional formats.[180]

In light of that data, if you're telling stories at a lifestyle brand, for instance, then TikTok might be a wise platform choice, along with Instagram, YouTube, or Facebook, and, of course, your brand's website or websites. By the same token, placing too much faith in one platform might cause you to miss reaching a lot of your brand's constituents.

Whatever content road you choose, keep your stories anchored in the brand's vision. Doing so can help your brand and your audience see the road ahead.

Cobbling It Together Like
Pinocchio's Geppetto

Earlier, I praised CBS News storyteller Steve Hartman. Let me say that while most of us don't possess the remarkable abilities that Hartman does, or work with such a talented production team, we all can strive to be like him in terms of storytelling prowess.

I don't know the mechanics of how Hartman goes about

telling stories, but I figure he realizes who the audience is for each story and who the characters should be in each story. In addition, he tells stories in an authentic, straightforward, exceedingly compelling manner.

But most significantly, Hartman conveys humanity in each story. Considering all the trials and tribulations we experience in this world, every piece of brand storytelling could benefit from a healthy dose of humanity.

Rounding out your storytelling with a dose of Hartman's compassion and humanity can make your content more appealing and, therefore, can captivate your audience. Each Hartman-like story you share keeps your audience invested in your brand.

STRIPPING IT DOWN

1. **Tell a compelling story.** Although not every piece of content must be scintillating, it should be interesting enough to maintain your audience's interest. You can inject interest, in part, by weaving real people into your brand's stories when possible.

2. **Know your brand.** Familiarize yourself with the brand. Being aware of what the brand does, who its audience is, and what you want people to know about your brand can help drive your brand's storytelling.

3. **Keep it simple.** Stick to an approach of being simple, but not simplistic, with your brand's storytelling. Don't talk above or below your audience.

4. **Be real.** No one likes phoniness. Try to be as authentic as you can in your storytelling. It'll make your brand more relatable.

5. **Choose the appropriate vehicles for storytelling.** While white papers and case studies might appeal to a B2B audience, they probably won't win over B2C consumers.

eight

EXPOSING THE WORLD TO YOUR CONTENT

AS A SOCIETY, we're fixated on beauty. A quick Google search turns up several rankings of the world's most beautiful women and the world's most beautiful destinations. So, it was only natural that LawnStarter, an outdoor services platform, would generate content related to outdoor beauty.

In 2017 when I was LawnStarter's editor in chief, I rounded up a list of the "14 Most Picturesque High School Campuses in the U.S."[181] That post was among a number of successful LawnStarter pieces I created that played on the "picturesque" theme. Those pieces consistently delivered the goods in terms of audience interaction.

The gorgeous bayside campus of Stadium High School in Tacoma, Washington, topped the 2017 list. I subjectively ranked schools based on a thorough Google review of photos highlighting high school campuses. Once we published the list on our website, I embarked on an effort to promote the rankings. I zeroed in on media outlets in the communities where the "picturesque" campuses were located. Outlets in the Seattle-Tacoma metro area were prime targets. But aside from mentions by media outlets, I was aiming for social media traffic on Facebook. I knew the list was a mega-shareable piece of content. The strategy worked.

The Facebook page of Stadium High School posted a link to LawnStarter's article about the rankings. The school's post drew 992 likes, 370 shares, and 63 comments.[182] Score! That social media engagement would benefit LawnStarter's website, as the link would generate web traffic. On top of that, the school's Facebook post could catch the attention of media outlets, which then might cite the LawnStarter rankings.

Regardless of whether you employ in-house or outsourced PR and social media teams, it's critical to promote your brand's content. Otherwise, your content might simply languish like a garden full of dead roses. That observation brings to mind the age-old question, "If a tree falls in a forest, and there's no one around to hear it, does it make a sound?"

Where's your forest? Research published in 2020 by the Content Marketing Institute shows that in the B2B world, email is the third most popular kind of content (81 percent), preceded by blog posts and short articles (89 percent), and social media (95 percent).[183]

By the way, you don't need to focus solely on email newsletters as a content marketing strategy, however successful those newsletters might be according to the Content Marketing Institute survey. Instead, it's best to bank on a mix of content promotion methods that suit your target audience. Some people won't subscribe to or open newsletters that you send, while others may never pay attention to LinkedIn posts.

To reach the most people possible, you must spread your content promotion across several platforms and freely promote content on the platforms where you can reach your audience in the most targeted way. For a B2B brand, that focus could be a combination of newsletters and LinkedIn. For a B2C brand, the effort might require a mix of Facebook, Instagram, and TikTok.

That being said, don't overlook any available avenue for promoting your content. What succeeds for your brand might not succeed for another brand. Experiment with different platforms (both free and paid), sticking with the ones that perform well and quickly moving on from the ones that fail.

The worst thing you can do in terms of promoting your content is to keep putting your faith in a platform that isn't delivering results in hopes that the tide will someday turn. You could be wasting valuable time waiting for an outcome that will never materialize.

How do you know your efforts are successful? Every brand measures success in different ways, but here are four signs:

1. The content generates an impressive number of likes, retweets, and so forth.

2. The content drives traffic to your website.

3. The content leads directly to sign-ups for your email newsletter and other positive actions.

4. The content sends people into your sales funnel.

By achieving those four measures of success, you can build out the content marketing platform that you planned for and dreamed of.

Adding Social Media to the Content Promotion Mix

Survey findings from Databox indicate social media reigns as the preferred method of content promotion, followed by email. In fact, marketers turn first to social media for content promotion before any other route, according to Databox.[184] Aside from using Facebook, marketers questioned by Databox report success with Twitter, LinkedIn, and Quora, among other platforms.

Content promotion is so critical that Jonathan Aufray, co-founder and CEO of Growth Hackers, an agency that specializes in digital marketing and lead generation, thinks 20 percent of your time should be spent on creating content and 80 percent on promoting it.[185]

While I'm not sure the 80/20 split can or should apply to every brand, I do believe that more time should be devoted to content promotion than to content creation. Still, you should never give short shrift to content creation. It's pretty tough to successfully promote terrible content.

In my tenure as a content marketing specialist, I've found that social media frequently pans out when it comes to content promotion. As I alluded to earlier, posts that LawnStarter published about the "most beautiful" or "prettiest" or "best" of something typically performed well on Facebook. Aside from the piece about high school campuses, posts that fell into this category included "The 16 College Football Stadiums With the

Best Natural Scenery"[186] and "The 9 Best College Football Fields With Good Ol' Grass."[187]

Why did those posts perform so well? Because people take pride in their local schools, their alma maters, or any other organizations that tug at their heartstrings. People love to brag that a school they attended (or attend) is the "best" in this or the "most" in that.

Plus, this family of unscientific, subjective rankings aligned with the LawnStarter brand. LawnStarter is all about improving the aesthetics around your home. So, why not zero in on schools and other places with eye-pleasing aesthetics? It didn't hurt that I was able to hunt down some dazzling photos of the properties featured in those rankings, although I must confess that the photo-finding process hogged a lot of my time.

But when you're talking about beauty, photos are the star. Pretty photos pop on social media platforms like Facebook, Instagram, and Pinterest. While I cut my professional teeth as a wordsmith, I realize the impact that a nice photo can have when you're trying to showcase your content on social media. (As a word guy, it hurts a little to say that photos matter just as much—if not more—than the words do when you're promoting content on social media.)

How to Kill It in Content Promotion

While I'm no content promotion guru, I must have spent hundreds of hours telling the world about content that I've helped produce. The experience has taught me a few lessons that I'd like to share with you.

1. **Realize that success goes hand in hand with failure.**

   Unfortunately, your target audience will not relate to every piece of content you promote. For every success you enjoy, you're likely to experience one failure. But rather than be dejected by failure, learn from it. Get the answers to these questions:

   → Did the content simply miss the mark?

   → Did your content promotion fall short?

   → What could you have done differently?

   In content marketing roles I've held, I haven't had the luxury of licking my wounds and brooding for days. I had to move on to promoting another piece of content. Just remember that even the best baseball players strike out. Hitters with batting averages above .400 are off-the-charts exceptional.

2. **Play around with different formats.**

   It's more than okay to experiment with content promotion. Perhaps you've never shared a piece of your brand's content on Pinterest, but you've generated some content that you think would attract interest on the image-sharing platform. Why not give that content a shot to shine on Pinterest? You never know when you might land on a platform that exceeds your expectations.

   We sometimes get stuck in ruts when we're sharing content on social media; stepping outside your social media comfort zone might pay off.

3. **Track your activity.**

To build on successes and avoid failures in content promotion, you must monitor the results.

At LawnStarter, we meticulously tracked the number of backlinks generated by each piece of content in a spreadsheet. It gave us a chance to celebrate the victories, reflect on the misses, and figure out which types of content are worth repeating (like the "beautiful" stadium or campus rankings) and which ones should be abandoned. Of course, you also can and should measure the success of content promotion by looking at metrics such as web traffic, content shares, and keyword rankings.[188]

At every place where I've overseen content marketing, I've obsessively studied Google Analytics trends for each piece of content. While I don't necessarily suggest being as captivated by Google Analytics as I've been, I do recommend paying close attention to what the statistics are telling you about the performance of your content.

The data can give you key insights into which types of content you should continue to produce and promote, and which types of content it might be time to ditch.

4. **Invest in content creation and promotion.**

The internet is loaded with terrible content. I come across drivel every day. As such, it's imperative that your brand produces content that rises well above the drivel. It doesn't need to be award-caliber, but it does need to be well-thought-out and well-crafted. Ferociously slapping together blog post after blog post after blog post won't serve your brand very well.

To steer clear of the dumpster full of internet garbage, you must adequately invest in content creation, whether that means an investment of time or money, or a combination of two. At LawnStarter, I lacked the financial resources to outsource content creation, so I had to do the best I could on my own with the time I had. My time, therefore, ended up being a valuable commodity. And I like to think that I excelled in that regard.

But just as important, if not more so, than content creation is content promotion. That, too, is an area where I feel as though I've put my best foot forward.

It sometimes takes days to gear up for promotion of a piece of content. At LawnStarter, that effort mostly meant a number of hours compiling media lists, emailing media contacts, and following up with media outlets that hadn't responded to my pitches. Dedicating so much time to media outreach and social media sharing helps ensure that whatever content I'm promoting stands the best chance possible of soaring.

At two previous employers, SpareFoot and Bankrate, I thankfully could depend on sizable content marketing budgets that allowed us to go down different paths, such as tapping an agency to produce and promote infographics and giving a raft of content assignments to freelance writers.

Wherever your brand is on the budget spectrum, just know that you can create and promote content that will not only trigger a sound in the forest but can make a big noise.

A shoestring operation can succeed in content creation and promotion. As long as you've sufficiently cultivated and tended to your content marketing garden, your work can yield a bumper crop of content marketing successes.

STRIPPING IT DOWN

1. **Promote your content.** Don't let your content languish. Attract eyes and ears by gaining media coverage about your content or pushing it out on social media, for instance.

2. **Weigh the value of a newsletter.** A regular email newsletter can attract a bigger audience for your content and can introduce more people to your brand.

3. **Stay on top of performance.** Keep track of how your content is doing in terms of metrics like social media likes and shares, sales leads, and email sign-ups.

4. **Examine successes and failures.** Content promotion should involve studying what has performed well and what has flopped. Such analysis helps determine what types of promotion you should continue and what types of promotion you should abandon.

5. **Try different formats.** Facebook may be your most successful platform for content promotion, but don't be shy about heading down other avenues. Feel free to experiment.

nine

LET A CONTENT ROADMAP BE YOUR GUIDE

WHEN I FIRST began driving, back in the late 1970s, motorists trusted maps and atlases to help navigate unfamiliar territory. For years, I always stashed a map or atlas somewhere in my car. But now, paper maps and paper atlases take a back seat to technology—specifically GPS. I can't recall the last time, as a motorist, that I depended on a non-electronic map (thanks, Siri!) to get me from Point A to Point B.

Regardless of the form they take, maps still guide us. Nowhere is that truer than in content marketing. To successfully carry out a content marketing strategy, we need a sense of direction—where have we been and where are we headed? As such, maps become as vital to content marketers as they do to motorists.

Content marketing maps need not be fixed, however. As you travel along the content marketing road, you'll need to adjust your route to account for things like the introduction of a new product or a shift in sales priorities. Your content marketing roadmap should be nimble, not rigid. Don't let what's already part of your roadmap put up a roadblock in terms of adapting to change.

Creating Your Content Marketing Roadmap

Particularly if you've never set up a content marketing roadmap, you might feel intimidated by undertaking its creation. Don't be apprehensive—the task isn't nearly as tough as you might imagine.

DivvyHQ, whose content marketing tools I've used, explains that a content marketing roadmap "should act as your compass as you navigate your way to delivering impactful content that converts."[189] Speaking of delivering a meaningful impact, it's worth noting that when you visit the DivvyHQ website, a pop-up may ask why you visited or whether you'd like to learn more about what the DivvyHQ "nerds" are up to. Such added features engage a reader more than static words on a webpage or blog can.

1. **Evaluate your content.**

   The first step in your journey toward devising a content marketing roadmap involves evaluating your current content. A content audit, as it's called, should take a deep dive into the amount and types of content you've got.

   More importantly, you should dig into the analytics to determine which content is performing well and which content is not performing well. Included in your content audit should be a look at your SEO strategy. For instance, which SEO keywords are you using now? Are they attracting the right traffic for your brand? Should you tweak your keywords to improve search results?

2. **Examine brand goals.**

Next, you should examine the goals of your brand:

→ Are you looking to capture 20 percent more folks in your sales funnel?

→ Do you want to boost your brand authority?

→ Are you hoping to lift revenue by 10 percent over the next year?

→ Do you want to build trust with your audience?

→ Are you eager to increase brand awareness?

Those goals should match what you wind up laying out in your content roadmap. What kinds of content and which content topics will move the needle in achieving those goals? Ultimately, the objective should be to make your brand even more successful, however you measure success.

As you're thinking through those first two moves, be sure to assess both your content strategy and your content plan. If you have neither of those, then you've got a blank slate. But if your strategy and plan are already in place, you should periodically study both of them to ensure they're meeting your current needs.

As DivvyHQ defines it, your content strategy centers

on "the vision that informs the essence of everything your brand creates."[190] The content plan spells out how you're going to execute on that strategy.

3.   **Choose avenues for sharing content.**

Avenues for sharing your content might include:

→   Blog or website

→   Social media channels

→   Paid promotion through vehicles such as Google Ads

→   Media outreach via public relations

→   Influencers, such as high-profile users of platforms like Instagram and TikTok

→   Email newsletters

Your budget and your human resources will dictate which avenues you select and how extensively you'll tap into various distribution channels.

4.   **Consider the buyer's journey.**

Before you publish or distribute any content, your brand should consider the buyer's journey.

DivvyHQ defines the buyer's journey as "segmenting your audience, defining the touch points, considering user intent and identifying pain points."[191] The journey comprises three stages: awareness, consideration, and decision.

During the awareness stage, a buyer recognizes a pain point, such as exploring how to streamline a cumbersome invoicing system.

After the awareness stage, a buyer enters the consideration stage. At this juncture, a buyer starts to hunt for ways to ease the pain point but isn't yet ready to select a specific solution.

Finally, the buyer goes into the decision stage. That stage is when the buyer is ready to buy a product or service that takes care of the pain point.

As you're cobbling together the buyer's journey, keep in mind the buyer persona. This persona generally characterizes your target buyer. It's not a specific person but, rather, a mash-up of the myriad traits of your target buyer. Of course, your brand may have more than one buyer persona, depending on the basket of products and services that you offer.

The persona or personae of your brand help dictate the types of content you produce and how that content is distributed.

5. **Measure the success of content.**

Finally, your roadmap should point you in the right direction in terms of gauging the success of your content.

Not every brand will incorporate the same metrics into this equation. For instance, when I worked at LawnStarter, the most important metric for measuring the success of content marketing was the number and quality of the backlinks we gained for each piece of content. We tracked those statistics in a spreadsheet. Your brand may not care much about backlinks.

But what measures should you zero in on regarding the return on investment from content marketing? A 2021 survey of B2C marketers by the Content Marketing Institute offers some clarity. Following are the top metrics those marketers reported tracking in order to measure content performance in the previous 12 months:

→ Website engagement (such as time spent on the site)—69 percent

→ Conversions (such as leads to sales)—67 percent

→ Website traffic (including pageviews and back-links)—65 percent

→ Email engagement (such as "open" rates for emails)—64 percent

→ Social media analytics (including follows and likes)—51 percent [192]

The list isn't a prescription for how your brand should measure the success of your content. Instead, it can help inform your decisions about metrics.

Scheduling Content Production and Distribution

Once you've established a content roadmap, you should create what's known as an editorial calendar.

That tool outlines in visual form the types of content you plan to create, who is tasked with creating that content, the deadlines for completing the content, what sort of art elements you want to accompany each piece of content, the publication dates for the content, and where the content will be promoted, among other duties. An editorial calendar might shape your content workflow on a daily, weekly, monthly, or annual basis.

Your editorial calendar also might align with the seasonality of your business.

For example, the self-storage industry typically reaches its annual peak of activity right after Memorial Day.[193] So, in the weeks leading up to that period, a self-storage operator might want to publish several timely blog posts about subjects like preparing your belongings for self-storage or packing for an in-state move.

Or, if you're a retail brand, you might look at generating email newsletters with content aimed at informing your subscribers about how to survive the holiday shopping season.

Your editorial calendar may also support the upcoming release of a suite of new software products or the pending launch of a new line of coffee beverages. Or the calendar might be filled with content that's paired with a set of first-quarter sales goals.

As you're crafting an editorial calendar, keep in mind that nothing on the calendar is permanent. For example, you might elect to scrap one piece of content in favor of another. Or you might need to reassign a piece of content from one writer to another.

More broadly, you might need to rapidly change gears, meaning your current content calendar is pretty much useless.

The COVID-19 pandemic emphasized the need to pivot quickly in order to produce content that addressed the global health crisis. In short order, several of my content marketing clients had to essentially throw out their editorial calendars to make room for pandemic-related content.

For example, one of my clients, the Society for Human Resource Management (SHRM), reversed course to produce loads of content regarding pandemic-fueled HR matters. For SHRM, I wrote articles such as "Workplace Violence May Jump During Return to Work"[194] and "CEOs and Workers Don't See Eye to Eye on Mental Health Assistance."[195] The pandemic spawned both of those topics.

Another of my clients, eyecare website All About Vision, also generated numerous pieces of content connected to the pandemic. Topics I covered included "Coronavirus: COVID and your eyes"[196] and "The COVID-19 vaccine: Will it affect your vision?"[197]

Aside from the ability to respond to unforeseen developments like the pandemic, an editorial calendar should offer the freedom to make alterations based on things like content metrics. Perhaps you recently published an infographic about backyard gardening that crushed it online, so you've decided to pour more resources into infographics touching on adjacent topics. Or maybe a blog post about mobile homes that you had hoped would explode online wound up fizzling, so you've chosen to back off on posts tied to that topic for the time being.

If you find yourself in the fizzle category rather than the sizzle category, don't fret. Chalk it up as a lesson learned. Incorporate the takeaways from a content flop into your content strategy and plan.

One of the core values at SpareFoot encouraged "failing quickly." You can apply that core value to your content marketing efforts. If a piece of content fails, don't spend much time wringing your hands—you can't resuscitate a dead body. Instead, move ahead quickly to what's next on your content calendar and stick the "failure" in the back of your brain for future reference.

Springing into Action

At LawnStarter, I established what I believe was a solid foundation for the content marketing machine. Jeff Herman, who holds the same position I did at LawnStarter, now runs that machine.

When Herman was an editor in the news business, seasons and news events largely drove his work. The editorial team at LawnStarter does pay attention to the seasonality of lawn care. For instance, the LawnStarter website published a collection of leaf-blower product reviews in the spring that later in the year ranked among the 10 most-read blog posts.

But the company doesn't rigidly stick to a season-based or full-year content marketing plan. Rather, the plan changes every quarter as LawnStarter sets new content goals. That objective could be something as basic as boosting a website's presence.

For example, LawnStarter purchased a rival, Lawn Love, in the summer of 2021.[198] At that point, Jeff and his team started zeroing in on producing lawn care articles to fill out Lawn Love's blog content. The company hired a managing editor to oversee the long-term effort; initial duties included coaching a handful of new writers. To supplement the cadre of new writers, some veteran LawnStarter writers were tapped for the Lawn Love team.

At the outset, Jeff and his teammates created content targeted at the largest Lawn Love markets. In many cases, such content informs local residents about subjects such as how to care for their lawns during the summer and what types of flowers, trees, bushes, and so forth to plant for their specific climates. SEO keywords guided the topics of those posts. Lawn Love writers even chipped in some content ideas.

Simultaneously, Jeff has spearheaded the publication of content tied to LawnStarter's expansion into outdoor services beyond lawn care, such as pest control and leaf removal. Furthermore, LawnStarter generates articles and guides designed to help LawnStarter's independent service professionals grow their businesses.

Much of the content is what's known as evergreen content. Evergreen content remains relevant regardless of the season or the time frame, never goes out to style, and continually appeals to people in search of answers to myriad questions.[199] It's designed to constantly draw organic traffic from Google and other search engines.

Evergreen content, and many other types of content, often include at least one call to action, encouraging the reader to engage with you. The message might direct a reader to sign up for a newsletter or to download a PDF-formatted report.

In addition to using evergreen content, LawnStarter hunts for places to publish guest posts about brand-connected topics (like lawn care) and invests in research to support an array of studies that may or may not be aligned directly with LawnStarter's services.

For example, in November 2021, LawnStarter published a

study ranking the best U.S. cities for remote workers.[200] A few days before, it published a study ranking the best U.S. cities for barbecue lovers.[201] The key goal of those studies is to gain backlinks from media outlets and to send traffic to the LawnStarter website. The strategy does yield results, although some writers, reporters, and editors still question why LawnStarter is pumping out studies about the top spots for remote work and barbecue.

You can use a project management platform, as LawnStarter does, to track all the moving editorial parts. And if you've adopted a flexible platform, you should be able to tailor it to your brand's particular needs. Here are examples of how you might silo your content:

→   Has been proposed

→   Has been assigned

→   Is being drafted

→   Is being edited and reviewed

→   Is being audited for SEO compatibility

→   Has been formatted and scheduled for publication

When combined, those elements form a full-fledged content calendar.

Creating and managing an editorial calendar keeps you organized and, just as importantly, keeps you focused on accomplishing your content goals and measuring your content's performance. Without that sort of structure, you risk traveling down the content road without any sort of map and losing your way.

Keeping It All Organized Like Martha Stewart

Overseeing a brand's content marketing—including your editorial calendar—can feel like trying to direct air traffic at Hartsfield-Jackson Atlanta International Airport, one of the world's busiest airports.[202] You've got a lot of stuff flying around you all at once. But there are ways to keep your sanity as well as to keep takeoffs and landings as smooth as possible.

Take the editorial calendar, for instance. The calendar should live somewhere that it can be shared among members of the content marketing team. The solution could be as elementary as maintaining the calendar in Google Sheets or using a content calendar template. To step it up a few notches, you can try calendar software from providers like HubSpot, Google, and WordPress.

For a more robust approach, look into project management tools from providers like Asana, ClickUp, monday.com, Trello, and Wrike.[203]

Trello happens to be my favorite among content management platforms. Trello (which didn't compensate me for lauding them) is used by LawnStarter and by GPO. "Trello is an eye-catching, fun, and intuitive app that helps you organize, coordinate, and track work," *PC Magazine* notes in a review of Trello.[204]

At Trello's core are Kanban "sticky note" workflow management boards that are ridiculously easy to maneuver. Trello does a fantastic job of scheduling, monitoring, and housing content. After testing several content management platforms, Trello remains my go-to whenever my work calls for tracking work through project management software.

Trello simplifies tracking, like a spreadsheet on steroids without the side effects. Haley Collins says she "can't say that there is anything I necessarily like or dislike" about Trello. "I went from using an Excel spreadsheet to Trello, so every feature was an upgrade."

Other technological marvels that might help you map and manage your content include:

→ **Analytics software.** To keep on top of how your content is performing, try technology like Ahrefs, Conductor, Google Analytics, and Parse.ly.

→ **Blogging platforms.** Your brand's blog posts must be hosted somewhere. Options include WordPress (my favorite), LinkedIn, and Medium.

→ **Email newsletter software.** Companies such as Constant Contact, HubSpot, Mailchimp, and Sendinblue provide email newsletter software.

→ **Image-creating tools.** Technology providers such as Canva, infogr.am, and Venngage[205] can put image wizardry in the hands of any content marketer, regardless of their graphic skills. I have often turned to infogr.am to produce sleek graphics fairly easily.

→ **Social media management platforms.** To oversee your brand's activity on social media in a cohesive fashion, consider employing tools such as Buffer, Hootsuite, and Sprout Social.[206]

→ **Title generators.** These tools can give you an edge when it comes to conceiving ideas for blog posts. They include

HubSpot's Blog Ideas Generator, Kickass Headline Generator, and Topic's Blog Idea Generator.[207]

→ **SEO help:**

- Clearscope.[208] This is an AI-powered tool that suggests SEO keywords and keyphrases for your content.

- Moz.[209] This software helps you improve various aspects of website SEO.

- Semrush. This software gives you a better handle on SEO keyword research and other digital marketing tasks.

- Slack. This tool makes it easier to communicate and collaborate with team members.

→ **Content ideas.** I frequently use Google to come up with content topics. Start typing words like "How to" or "What can I" and see what pops up in your search. That simple activity can help you develop all sorts of content that answers questions frequently asked by internet users.

→ **Analytics.** Google Trends is a handy-dandy website that analyzes the popularity of Google search queries. For me, it's proven to be great fodder for content ideas.

Whatever technology you choose to help steer your editorial process, be sure to choose what works for you. Perhaps you and your team are satisfied with sticking to good old spreadsheets, particularly if you have no money to purchase technology. If you do have the budget for a tech-powered system, you can easily mix and match elements that suit your needs and collectively streamline your process.

Regardless of what your setup looks like, just remember to incorporate flexibility into your content marketing operation and embrace trying new things, then dumping those things if they don't succeed and replicating them if they do succeed.

STRIPPING IT DOWN

1. **Evaluate your content.** An audit of your current storehouse of content and the content analytics can help you develop a roadmap for your content marketing program.

2. **Select your content-sharing routes.** Decide whether blogging or social media, for instance, should be key mile markers for your content roadmap.

3. **Examine the buyer's journey.** Look at the various buying stages that members of your audience go through.

4. **Pick ways to measure content success.** You may wind up concentrating on web traffic as a key metric, for instance, while mostly ignoring lead-to-sales conversions.

5. **Create an editorial calendar.** An editorial calendar outlines what pieces of content you plan to produce and when they will be published. Like your own personal calendar, it keeps you organized and helps you achieve your goals.

ten

CONTENT MARKETING IS NOT A CABBAGE PATCH KID

FADS COME AND go. Back in the 1980s, we had Cabbage Patch Kids, Rubik's Cube, "preppies," and myriad other fads.

In the mid-'80s, I remember being assigned an article for the student newspaper at the University of Kansas about whether the Ivy League-influenced preppy look—celebrated in movies like *Risky Business* and *Sixteen Candles*—was in or out. If I recall correctly, preppy-ism was somewhere between in and out at that time. Now, of course, it's a style that has been relegated mostly to '80s-era yearbooks, TV shows, and movies.

A Google search for the phrase "Is content marketing a fad?" turns up several articles regarding whether content marketing will go the way of preppy style. My belief is that content marketing, in some form, is not going away—and John Deere's enduring success with content marketing reaffirms that belief. In other words, it's not a fad that will fade away. However, I am sure various fads within content marketing will continue to vanish and new ones will appear.

As you contemplate your organization's approach to content marketing, I urge you to not dismiss content marketing as a fad. Doing so could push your brand onto the endangered species list, like the Izod shirt or popped-up shirt collar.

Rather than nearing extinction, your brand should "rinse and repeat" those content marketing tactics that have proven to be successful, drop those tactics that have sputtered, and latch onto emerging trends. The analytics tools you're using (or you should be using) can help guide decisions.

So, what does the future hold for content marketing?

I'm not able to gaze into a crystal ball and forecast the future, but I can point you in what I think is the right direction. Many of these elements pull from topics that I covered in previous chapters.

SEO

If my clients are any indication, SEO remains even more important than ever. I make that assessment based on the instructions I receive from them for content marketing assignments, such as blog posts.

By and large, my clients have stepped up their commitment to SEO. Increasingly, they provide lists of recommended keywords and semantically related keywords to drive the wording of content assignments. Some even employ tools to grade content based on the volume of targeted keywords and other SEO-related factors.

Bottom line: Content I produce for clients is more SEO

driven than I can recall.

Accuracy

Several of my content marketing clients are more meticulous than ever when it comes to accuracy. A prime example: A number of clients insist that outside information included in blog posts, articles, and other content be obtained from reliable sources. Those sources include .gov and .edu websites. Those sources do not, however, include Wikipedia or its online cousins.

In addition, several of my clients require that I find the original source of a study or survey if I'm citing it in a piece of content, rather than relying on a website that quoted the study or survey. They rightfully want to rely on firsthand, rather than secondhand, information.

It's heartening to see so many of my content marketing clients follow a rigorous approach to ensuring accuracy. That approach has its roots in the journalistic standards that I learned in college.

Sadly, though, that approach has faded in the mainstream media as their human resources have been decimated, particularly the vanishing breed of copy editors. (I was among them back in my newspaper days.) Inaccuracies big and small appear all the time in online content, a sign that speed in many cases has overtaken accuracy in importance.

In this contentious era of "fake news," it's more vital than ever to ensure content is as accurate as it can be.

Webinars

When the COVID-19 pandemic swept across the world, it shut the door on almost every in-person business gathering you can think of. In reaction to the crisis, many businesses shifted to delivering information via webinars rather than at in-person events. Sure, webinars have long been a facet of business communication, but I believe they will become even more of a fixture going forward.

Data released in 2021 by ON24, a San Francisco company that offers a "digital experience platform," shows that the use of webinars jumped 162 percent and that attendance nearly quadrupled in 2020 compared with the previous year. During the same period, webinar audiences engaged with more than 61 million hours of content, up nearly 300 percent.[210]

While the use of webinars could decline in the post-pandemic period, I think too many folks have gotten hooked on webinars for people to entirely lose interest in them.

Webinars are here to stay, and content marketing teams should determine whether they should add webinars to their lineups or boost their current webinar activity.

Dynamic Content

As artificial intelligence and machine learning become even more commonplace, content marketers should be prepared to crank up their involvement in dynamic content. Omniconvert, a provider of marketing software, defines dynamic content as web and email content that changes based on a user's behavior, preferences, and interests.[211]

One of my clients, content marketing agency GPO, is producing more and more dynamic content. In fact, GPO's Haley Collins tells me that dynamic content is the next big thing in content marketing. If Haley's prediction is accurate, and I believe it is, then content marketers should add dynamic content to their vocabulary.

As you continue to negotiate the ever-shifting landscape of content marketing, let me leave you with some final thoughts based on what I've covered thus far.

Adopting a Journalist Mindset

Content marketing is not advertising, PR, or traditional marketing. Rather, content marketing involves producing and sharing content, in a variety of forms, that connects with your target audience. I believe it should be viewed as marketing infused with the DNA of journalism.

If you consistently inject a journalistic mindset into your content, your brand's blog posts, e-books, infographics, and the like will shine.

Embracing a "Scrappy" Attitude

You've undoubtedly heard of "scrappy" start-ups. They are young businesses that lack the resources and brand recognition of major companies.

Overseeing content marketing at a scrappy start-up (LawnStarter) taught me—actually, forced me—to be creative and resourceful. That mindset can benefit you, regardless of whether you're working on content marketing at a small or big brand. Instead of whining about what you're unable to do because of strained resources, focus on what you can do with what you've got.

The results will likely surprise you, stretch your capabilities, and very well could yield the outcomes you hoped for.

Building Your Brand's Authority

Never overlook the impact that a well-crafted content marketing strategy can have on your brand's authority. That being said, keep in mind that in the quest for brand authority, the time and energy you allocate for your brand's content marketing matters more than how much money you throw at the strategy.

While building your brand's authority via content marketing takes hard work and stick-to-itiveness, it can be immensely worthwhile.

Getting Up to Speed with SEO

To succeed in content marketing, you must familiarize yourself with three letters: SEO. Broadly speaking, SEO (search engine optimization) is designed to make your online content more appealing to search engines (namely, Google) and ultimately draw more traffic to your website. Whenever you're considering the topics and types of content to post online, SEO should always be a key factor.

While you don't want to overload your content with SEO-friendly keywords, you also don't want to skimp on SEO. Vital to the balance are effort and expertise. Expertise could come in the form of an in-house specialist dedicated to SEO or an outside SEO agency. Or you could teach yourself enough about SEO so you can pilot your brand's SEO ship.

In the end, make sure SEO constitutes one of the most important threads of your content marketing efforts. Otherwise, that tapestry could unravel.

Developing Pillar Content

Pillars support many of the world's grandest structures, and they also support content marketing. A piece of pillar content, which typically is lengthy and links to related subtopics on your website, aims to answer questions that online searchers pose.

For instance, someone might type "What is pillar content?" into a search engine, and several well-rounded articles from highly regarded websites pop up in the search results. Such in-depth guides on an array of topics relevant to your brand can drive tons of web traffic as well as lift your website's standing in the eyes of Google's algorithms. Relevant content should be one of the pillars of your approach to content marketing.

Appreciating the Value of Blogging

Speaking of pillars, the tried-and-true blog post remains one of the most popular and most effective types of content marketing. Among other things, blog posts can drive robust web traffic, boost customer outreach and engagement, and be published and updated on a regular basis. In addition, a blog post can be someone's first introduction to your brand.

No matter what else you tackle in your content marketing program, blogging should always remain at the core. A content marketing initiative without blogging is like a sailboat without a rudder. You can steer a rudder-less sailboat, but the lack of a rudder makes the job much tougher.

Remembering Your Brand's Story

As you assess your approach to content marketing, always keep in mind your brand's story. Yes, every brand has a story to tell. While it might not be as scintillating as a James Patterson novel, your brand's story matters.

To properly convey your brand's story, you need to nail down the narrative. What makes your brand stand out? What drives your organization's success? What emotion(s) does your brand evoke?

You can tap into the answers to those questions (and others) to mold your brand's story and then tell it via whatever vehicle makes sense—videos, blog posts, white papers, and so forth.

Never lose sight of the storytelling pillar of your brand. Everyone loves good stories, and your brand story can be among those telling them.

Immersing Your Brand in Storytelling

When you think of great storytellers, who comes to mind? Perhaps William Shakespeare. Or maybe Charles Dickens. When you're crafting your brand's story, borrow a page from their book: They rivet their readers with compelling plots and fascinating characters.

Chances are your brand's story isn't material for a best-selling novel. However, you should still imbue your brand's story with elements that capture an audience's attention. Yes, industries like self-storage and lawn care can be boring—trust me on that one—but your brand's story need not be dull.

If you want folks to pay attention to your brand, you must captivatingly yet authentically tell your brand's story.

Attracting an Audience

Whatever sort of content you're producing to support your brand, you must draw eyeballs (or ears) to it. Otherwise, it's simply not worth the effort and expense. This is where content promotion comes in.

Content promotion can be in the form of email newsletters, social media posts, and media outreach, to name a few methods. No matter which content promotion methods you pick, know that promotion can consume just as much time—if not more—than creating content can. And that's the way it should be. You can't assume that if you build great content, they will come (a twist on the often-repeated quote from the movie *Field of Dreams*).

If you build great content, you must put out the welcome mat for your audience.

Navigating the World of Content Marketing

Would you set out on a cross-country trip without a digital or paper map? Unless you're trying to get lost, you should depend on a map to help guide you. You're wise to adopt the same mindset when it comes to content marketing.

Your content marketing map should include guideposts like your brand's goals, your editorial calendar, and your tools for measuring the success of your content. The map can be loosely or tightly structured, but it is key to develop that map so you don't veer off your content marketing path.

Showing 'Em What You've Got

No one pointed me to a book like this when I set out on my ongoing journey in content marketing. It's my hope that this book better equips you to venture into content marketing or beef up your content marketing initiatives.

Regardless of whether you work at a scrappy start-up or a colossal company, forge ahead with the belief that you can accomplish more with content marketing than you probably ever envisioned. And march forward with the understanding that trial and error can be one of your best friends, not one of your fiercest enemies.

You never know when your brand's own World Naked Gardening Day experiment can uncover what your brand's content marketing program is capable of growing.

ACKNOWLEDGEMENTS

WOW. THERE ARE so many folks to thank for their support in getting this book out of my head and into print. And I know I'm going to fail to mention some of them. But here goes ...

Thanks to Haley Collins and Jeff Herman for reviewing a pre-editing version of this book and offering valuable feedback.

Thanks to my teachers in the Olathe, Kansas, school system and my professors at Johnson County Community College (Overland Park, Kansas), the University of Kansas and Southern New Hampshire University for helping me hone my skills and helping me become a lifelong learner.

Thanks to former bosses like Ryan Farley of LawnStarter (quoted in this book), Brian Megless (formerly of SpareFoot and also quoted in this book) and Dan Ray (formerly of Bankrate) for their professional encouragement.

Thanks to my clients for their continued faith in me.

Thanks to my fellow content entrepreneurs for their guidance and inspiration.

Thanks to my family and friends for being there for me.

Thanks to everybody at Book Launchers for holding my hand throughout the process of writing my first book and, most importantly, for making this book better than I ever could have imagined.

I'd love to hear more about your own World Naked Gardening
Day triumphs and your other content marketing efforts!

REACH OUT!

johnegan.net

linkedin.com/in/johnjegan

ENDNOTES

1   Arnie Kuenn, "Is John Deere the Original Content Marketer?" Mar-Tech, June 25, 2013, https://martech.org/is-john-deere-the-original-content-marketer/.

2   "About The Furrow," John Deere, accessed March 15, 2022, https://www.deere.com/en/publications/the-furrow/.

3   "John Deere's The Furrow Magazine Launches Podcast," Crop Producer, April 30, 2019, https://cropproducer.com/john-deeres-the-furrow-magazine-launches-podcast/.

4   Kate Gardiner, "The Story Behind 'The Furrow,' The World's Oldest Content Marketing," Contently, October 3, 2013, https://contently.com/2013/10/03/the-story-behind-the-furrow-2/.

5   Dean Houghton, "Plowing a Straight Furrow," The Furrow, January 1, 2021, https://www.deere.com/en/publications/the-furrow/2021/january-2021/plowing-a-straight-furrow/.

6   Minda Smiley, "John Deere, the 'OG Content Marketer,' on How Its 123-year-old Magazine Endures," The Drum, https://www.thedrum.com/news/2018/05/24/john-deere-the-og-content-marketer-how-its-123-year-old-magazine-endures.

7   "What Is 'Content Marketing Strategy' in 2020?" Global Reach, June 25, 2020, https://www.globalreach.com/global-reach-media/blog/2020/06/25/what-is-content-marketing-strategy-in-2020.

8   Julia McCoy, "Was John Deere the First Proponent of Content Marketing? The Story That Started in 1895," Express Writers, April 12, 2017, https://expresswriters.com/the-story-of-john-deere-and-content-marketing/.

9   "David Jones: The Original Content Marketers—John Deere and 'The Furrow' [#CMWorld Recap]," Content Marketing World, December 18, 2014, https://www.contentmarketingworld.com/david-jones-original-content-marketers-john-deere-furrow-cmworld-recap/.

10   "Content Marketing Industry Report," ResearchDive, accessed March 18, 2022, https://www.researchdive.com/118/content-market.

11   Lalit Sharma, "5 Content Marketing Mistakes You Should Never Commit," Social Media Today, October 12, 2017, https://www.socialmediatoday.com/news/5-content-marketing-mistakes-you-should-never-commit/507050/.

12   "5 Essential Tips for a Successful Content Marketing Strategy," Digital Marketing Institute, January 15, 2018, https://digitalmarketinginstitute. com/blog/5-essential-tips-for-a-successful-content-marketing-strategy.

13   "Content Marketing: The Ultimate Beginner's Guide," Search Engine Journal, accessed March 18, 2022, https://www.searchenginejournal. com/content-marketing/what-is-content-marketing/#close.

14   Kristen Shipley and Abby Loar, "Crisis Marketing: How Brands Are Addressing The Coronavirus," Think With Google, April 2020, https:// www.thinkwithgoogle.com/future-of-marketing/digital-transformation/ coronavirus-crisis-marketing-examples/.

15   Ask a Pharmacist by Walgreens YouTube page, accessed March 20, 2022, https://www.youtube.com/channel/UCz_tzS7duKxWRK8ii98bZDA.

16   "Mobile Content Marketing Strategy," Izea, February 16, 2018, https:// izea.com/resources/mobile-content-marketing-strategy/.

17   Sharon Hurley Hall, "31 Impressive Content Marketing Examples You Can Use Today," Optin Monster, July 27, 2021, https://optinmonster. com/content-marketing-examples/.

18   Olivia Gochnour, "Content Cadence and Why It's Important," Tiled, October 25, 2019, https://www.tiled.co/blog/content-cadence-andwhy-its-important.

19   Alex DiRenzo, "Infographic: The Importance of Consistency in Content Marketing," July 16, 2019, https://www.shutterstock.com/blog/ consistency-content-marketing.

20   Nayomi Chibana, "10 Ways to Do Content Marketing in Boring Industries," Visme, October 21, 2015, https://visme.co/blog/content-marketing-boring-industries/.

21   "Landscaping Services Industry in the US - Market Research Report," August 23, 2021, https://www.ibisworld.com/united-states/market-research-reports/landscaping-services-industry/.

22   John Egan, "The Top 12 U.S. Cities for Observing World Naked Gardening Day," LawnStarter, May 6, 2021, https://www.LawnStarter.com/blog/gardening-2/world-naked-gardening-day/.

23   "5 Reasons NOT to Get Naked in Miami on Naked Gardening Day," *Miami Herald,* May 3, 2016, https://www.miamiherald.com/news/local/community/miami-dade/article75274417.html.

24   LawnStarter, "In cased [sic] you missed it, LawnStarter's very own John Egan was featured on the Weather channel. See what he has to say about 2016's World Naked Gardening day!" Facebook, May 23, 2016, https://www.facebook.com/LawnStarter/posts/in-cased-you-missed-it-LawnStarters-very-own-john-egan-was-featured-on-the-weath/1106480452728459/.

25   "Editor in Chief (Head of Content) Job," Lensa, accessed March 18, 2022, https://lensa.com/editor-in-chief-head-of-content-jobs/austin/jd/764bc76965f9af5e6f8cb12f237f18cc.

26   Sujan Patel, "How LawnStarter Hit Double-Digit Growth Through Creative Marketing," Inc.com, accessed March 20, 2022, https://www.inc.com/sujan-patel/how-LawnStarter-hit-double-digit-growth-through-creative-marketing.html.

27   Ibid.

28   Kathryn Hawkins, "What you'll learn about clickbait could shock you (don't miss #3)," Keap, updated June 10, 2021, https://keap.com/business-success-blog/marketing/content-marketing/what-is-clickbait.

29   Sujan Patel, "An Interview with Ryan Farley: How Being Scrappy Propelled LawnStarter to Success," *Forbes,* September 25, 2016, https://www.forbes.com/sites/sujanpatel/2016/09/25/interview-with-ryan-farley/?sh=77b4fbd16b13.

30   Aaron Agius, "How Much Should Your Company Budget for Content Marketing?" *Forbes,* January 20, 2021, https://www.forbes.com/sites/forbesagencycouncil/2021/01/20/how-much-should-your-company-budget-for-content-marketing.

31   "B2B Content Marketing 2020," Content Marketing Institute, accessed March 18, 2022, https://contentmarketinginstitute.com/wp-content/uploads/2019/10/2020_B2B_Research_Final.pdf.

32   Ibid.

33   John Egan, "America's Love Affair With Bedrooms and Bathrooms [Infographic]," LawnStarter, December 26, 2016, https://www.lawnstarter.com/blog/home-garden/bedroom-and-bathroom-trends/.

34   John Egan, "Kansas City Metro Leads the Way for Big Home Lots," LawnStarter, January 16, 2017, https://www.lawnstarter.com/kansas-city-mo-lawn-care/home-lot-sizes-in-kansas-city.

35   John Egan, "The 14 Most Maxed-Out Metros for Housing Debt," LawnStarter, April 14, 2020, https://www.lawnstarter.com/blog/city-rankings/metro-areas-housing-debt/.

36   John Egan, "The 9 Finest Grass Fields in Minor League Baseball," LawnStarter, December 26, 2016, https://www.lawnstarter.com/blog/lawn-care-2/minor-league-baseball-best-fields/.

37   John Hickey, "Turf Battle in the NFL: Natural vs. Artificial," LawnStarter, March 2, 2022, https://www.lawnstarter.com/blog/lawn-care-2/turf-at-nfl-stadiums/.

38   John Egan, "Report Card: The 14 Most Picturesque High School Campuses in the U.S.," LawnStarter, October 15, 2019, https://www.lawnstarter.com/blog/landscaping/prettiest-high-school-campuses/.

39   "What Is Domain Authority?" BigCommerce, accessed March 16, 2022, https://www.bigcommerce.com/ecommerce-answers/what-is-domain-authority/.

40   John Egan, "How Windy Is Tallahassee? [Infographic]," March 7, 2017, https://www.LawnStarter.com/tallahassee-fl-lawn-care/windy-weather-tallahassee-infographic.

41   Alexander Harris, "Tech Firms Combine Under Storable Brand Name to Serve Self-Storage Industry," SpareFoot Storage Beat, June 24, 2019, https://www.sparefoot.com/self-storage/news/8148-tech-firms-combine-storable-brand-name-serve-self-storage-industry/.

42   Jen Wilson, "CreditCards.com Owner Bankrate Agrees to $1.4 Billion Buyout," *Austin Business Journal,* updated July 5, 2017, https://www.bizjournals.com/austin/news/2017/07/03/creditcards-com-owner-bankrate-agrees-to-1-4.html.

43   Ibid.

44 "John Egan," Bankrate.com, accessed March 20, 2022, https://www.bankrate.com/authors/john-egan/.

45 Alexander Harris, "U.S. Self-Storage Industry Statistics," SpareFoot Storage Beat, January 27, 2021, https://www.sparefoot.com/self-storage/news/1432-self-storage-industry-statistics/.

46 John Egan, "Forecast: Self-Storage Revenue to Pass $30B in 2018," SpareFoot Storage Beat, May 27, 2015, https://www.sparefoot.com/self-storage/news/1443-storage-revenue-to-pass-30-billion-in-2018/.

47 John Egan, "Storage Operators Regroup After Hurricane Strikes," SpareFoot Storage Beat, September 25, 2017, https://www.sparefoot.com/self-storage/news/5919-storage-operators-regroup-after-hurricanes-strike/.

48 "Alexander Harris, Editor," SpareFoot Storage Beat, accessed March 20, 2022, https://www.sparefoot.com/self-storage/news/about-us/.

49 "SpareFoot Moving Guide," SpareFoot Moving Guides, accessed March 20, 2022, https://www.sparefoot.com/moving/about/.

50 John Egan, "National Real Estate Investor," John Egan.net, http://johnegan.net/portfolio/nrei/.

51 Barbara Bellesi Zito, "'National Real Estate Investor' Changed Its Name: What Investors Should Know," MillionAcres, December 22, 2020, https://www.millionacres.com/real-estate-basics/articles/national-real-estate-investor-changed-its-name-what-investors-should-know/.

52 Robert Evans, "How a Real Estate Blog Went From 2,000 to 18,000,000 Visits Per Month in Two Years," Movoto by OJO, December 10, 2014, https://www.movoto.com/blog/how-a-real-estate-blog-went-from-2000-to-18000000-visits-per-month-in-two-years/.

53 Lindsay Kolowich Cox, "The Best Infographics of 2014 (So Far)," HubSpot, accessed March 18, 2022, https://blog.hubspot.com/marketing/best-infographics-2014.

54 Molly St. Louis, "How to Spot Visual, Auditory, and Kinesthetic-Learning Executives," Inc., accessed March 18, 2022, https://www.inc.com/molly-reynolds/how-to-spot-visual-auditory-and-kinesthetic-learni.html.

55 Brian Nuckols, "29 Infographic Statistics You Need to Know in 2022," Visme, accessed March 18, 2022, https://visme.co/blog/infographic-statistics/.

56   Kai Tomboc, "Text vs. Images: Which Content Format is Effective?"
      May 30, 2019, Easelly, https://www.easel.ly/blog/text-vs-imag-
      es-which-content-format-effective/

57   Anant Patel, "12 Reasons Why Infographics Still Matter in SEO,"
      Semrush Blog, September 4, 2020, https://www.semrush.com/blog/12-
      reasons-why-infographics-still-matter-in-seo/.

58   "Why Infographics Are So Effective." Miss Details, accessed March 17,
      2022, https://missdetails.com/infographics-effective/.

59   "About NowSourcing," NowSourcing, accessed March 17, 2022,
      https://nowsourcing.com/about/.

60   John Egan, "Infographic: Portland vs. Austin – Which One Is the
      Weirdest?" SpareFoot Blog, March 14, 2014, https://www.sparefoot.
      com/self-storage/blog/5625-portland-vs-austin-weird-infographic/.

61   Ibid.

62   Andy Giegerich, "Which City Is Keeping It Weirder: Portland or
      Austin?" *Portland Business Journal,* March 18, 2014, https://www.
      bizjournals.com/portland/morning_call/2014/03/which-city-is-keeping-
      it-weirder-portland-or.html.

63   Nicole Cordier, "Weird War III: Portland Rising," Portland Month-
      ly, April 3, 2014, https://www.pdxmonthly.com/travel-and-out-
      doors/2014/04/the-battle-of-weird-april-2014.

64   "Keep Portland Weird," Wikipedia, updated December 11, 2021,
      https://en.wikipedia.org/wiki/Keep_Portland_Weird.

65   "Battle to Be the Weirdest City in America," New Zealand Herald, Au-
      gust 9, 2017, https://www.nzherald.co.nz/travel/battle-to-be-the-weird-
      est-city-in-america/K737OA4MEKPWHMWF3NWUQUW6HQ/.

66   Amy Campbell, "Crazy Tuesday Is Coming! Is Your Self-Storage Facility
      Prepared?" Inside Self-Storage, May 23, 2021, https://www.insideself-
      storage.com/crazy-tuesday-coming-your-self-storage-facility-prepared.

67   "5 Common Moving Mistakes – And How to Avoid Them," Today,
      May 28, 2014, https://www.today.com/home/5-common-moving-mis-
      takes-how-avoid-them-2D79721671.

68   Cristen James, "Meet August Luncheon Speaker, John Egan," Wom-
      en Communicators of Austin, August 3, 2014, https://wcaustin.
      org/2014/08/03/meet-august-luncheon-speaker-john-egan/.

69   John Egan, "We're a Winner: SpareFoot Earns Award for Blog Covering
      Self-Storage Industry," SpareFoot Blog, June 24, 2014, https://www.
      sparefoot.com/self-storage/blog/6443-sparefoot-wins-pr-daily-award/.

70   Barry Adams, "How to Get into Google News," Moz, January 11, 2019, https://moz.com/blog/how-to-get-into-google-news.

71   John Shehata, "Google News SEO – Everything Publishers Need to Know," accessed March 21, 2022, https://www.newzdash.com/guide/google-news-optimization-news-seo.

72   Amanda Milligan, "6 Ways to Build Brand Authority with Content Marketing," Moz, November 16, 2020, https://moz.com/blog/build-brand-authority-with-content-marketing.

73   Ibid.

74   Ibid.

75   Julia McCoy, "How to Build Your Brand's Authority with Strategic Content & SEO," Search Engine Journal, September 17, 2019, https://www.searchenginejournal.com/build-authority-strategic-content-seo/323139/#close.

76   Ben Johnson, "LawnStarter's Road from TechStars to Leading Lawn Marketplace," Proof, accessed March 20, 2022, https://blog.useproof.com/ryan-farley-LawnStarter.

77   Ellen Kriz, "Lawn Care Scheduling Platform to Add Pest Control Services," Pest Management Professional, November 13, 2019, https://www.mypmp.net/2019/11/13/lawn-care-scheduling-platform-to-add-pest-control-services/.

78   "Irrelevant Keywords," Google Search Central, lasted updated February 8, 2022, https://developers.google.com/search/docs/advanced/guidelines/irrelevant-keywords.

79   Caroline Forsey, "The Beginner's Guide to Keyword Density," HubSpot, updated May 5, 2022, https://blog.hubspot.com/marketing/keyword-density.

80   "Domain Authority," Moz, accessed March 17, 2022, https://moz.com/learn/seo/domain-authority.

81   Eric Siu, "5 Steps to Developing Successful Pillar Content," Single Grain, accessed March 18, 2022, https://www.singlegrain.com/blog-posts/content-marketing/5-steps-to-developing-successful-pillar-content/.

82   "How to Create Powerful Foundational Blog Content," Serve No Master, accessed March 18, 2022, https://servenomaster.com/how-to-create-powerful-foundational-blog-content/.

83   Ibid.

84 Eric Siu, "5 Steps to Developing Successful Pillar Content," Single Grain, accessed March 18, 2022, https://www.singlegrain.com/blog-posts/content-marketing/5-steps-to-developing-successful-pillar-content/.

85 John Egan, "Everything You Need to Know About How to Start a Self-Storage Business," Storable, July 26, 2021, https://www.storable.com/resources/learn/starting-a-self-storage-business/.

86 Eric Siu, "5 Steps to Developing Successful Pillar Content," Single Grain, accessed March 18, 2022, https://www.singlegrain.com/blog-posts/content-marketing/5-steps-to-developing-successful-pillar-content/.

87 Neil Patel, "Growth Hacking Made Simple: A Step-by-Step Guide," NeilPatel.com, accessed March 18, 2022, https://neilpatel.com/what-is-growth-hacking/.

88 Elise Dopson, "How to Get Ranked and Read with a Topic Cluster Model," Content Marketing Institute, updated January 11, 2021, https://contentmarketinginstitute.com/2021/01/ranked-topic-cluster-model/.

89 Elise Dopson, "21 Examples of High-Performing Pillar Pages to Draw Inspiration from," Databox, June 17, 2021, https://databox.com/examples-of-high-performing-pillar-pages.

90 Scott Yates, "5 Ideas for Creating Killer Evergreen Content [+Examples]," HubSpot, accessed March 18, 2022, https://blog.hubspot.com/insiders/creating-evergreen-content.

91 John Egan, "Credit Karma Guide to Finances for Newlyweds," Credit Karma, updated October 27, 2021, https://www.creditkarma.com/advice/i/credit-karma-guide-to-finances-for-newlyweds.

92 John Egan, "Credit Karma Guide to Budgeting," Credit Karma, February 4, 2022, https://www.creditkarma.com/advice/i/credit-karma-guide-budgeting.

93 Elise Dopson, "21 Examples of High-Performing Pillar Pages to Draw Inspiration from," Databox, June 17, 2021, https://databox.com/examples-of-high-performing-pillar-pages.

94 Ibid.

95 "Main Street Hub Featured by AustInnovation," Medium.com, November 14, 2015, https://medium.com/main-street-hub/main-street-hub-featured-by-austinnovation-d302708c5660.

96   Salkin, Miné. "40+ Content Marketing Statistics to Power Your 2022 Strategy." Semrush Blog, March 29, 2022. https://www.semrush.com/blog/content-marketing-statistics/; Semrush, ed. "The State of Content Marketing 2022 Global Report." Semrush Blog. Accessed August 4, 2022. https://www.semrush.com/state-of-content-marketing/success/.

97   BrightEdge, ed. "Why Should I Blog?" BrightEdge. Accessed August 4, 2022. https://www.brightedge.com/glossary/why-you-should-be-blogging.

98   Alexa Collins, "Build Your Brand: 8 Ecommerce Blog Examples for Better Content Marketing," Shopify Blog, October 22, 2021, https://www.shopify.com/blog/blog-examples.

99   BioLite's main page, accessed March 20, 2022, https://www.bioliteenergy.com.

100 "Why Blog? Statistics Show the Benefits," Marketpath, accessed March 18, 2022, https://webservices.marketpath.com/digital-marketing-insights/why-blog-statistics-show-the-benefits.

101 Julia McCoy, "53 Blogging Statistics That Prove a Blog Is Worth Your Time," Express Writers, September 1, 2020, https://expresswriters.com/blogging-statistics/.

102 Ibid.

103 "How to Start a Blog for Business: 13 Experts Weigh in on Benefits of Blogging," Omnicore, January 4, 2022, https://www.omnicoreagency.com/how-to-start-a-blog-for-business/.

104 Kyle Byers, "Content Marketing Case Study: How I Got 843% More Traffic from 1 Blog Post," GrowthBadger, August 2, 2019, https://growthbadger.com/double-survey-technique/.

105 Ibid.

106 John Egan, "Which Areas Employ the Most Lawn Care in the U.S.?" LawnStarter, March 11, 2017, https://www.LawnStarter.com/blog/landscaping/areas-with-the-most-lawn-care-workers/.

107 John Egan, "Everything You Need to Know About How to Start a Self-Storage Business," Storable, July 26, 2021, https://www.storable.com/resources/learn/starting-a-self-storage-business/.

108 John Egan, "17 New Year's Resolutions to Help You Get Organized," SpareFoot Blog, January 2, 2020, https://www.sparefoot.com/self-storage/blog/5032-new-years-resolutions-for-getting-organized/.

109 John Egan, "Before and After: 4 Great Decluttering Success Stories," SpareFoot Blog, November 6, 2014, https://www.sparefoot.com/self-storage/blog/7049-decluttering-success-stories/.

110 Alexander Harris, "U.S. Self-Storage Industry Statistics," SpareFoot Storage Beat, January 27, 2021, https://www.sparefoot.com/self-storage/news/1432-self-storage-industry-statistics/.

111 John Egan, "Self-Storage Industry Reacts to the Coronavirus Pandemic," SpareFoot Storage Beat, March 18, 2020, https://www.sparefoot.com/self-storage/news/9211-self-storage-industry-reacts-to-the-coronavirus-pandemic/.

112 John Egan, "California Storage Owners Face Potentially 'Disastrous' Tax Hike," SpareFoot Storage Beat, November 19, 2018, https://www.sparefoot.com/self-storage/news/7413-california-storage-owners-face-potentially-disastrous-tax-hike/.

113 Pamela Vaughan, "12 Revealing Charts to Help You Benchmark Your Business Blogging Performance [NEW DATA]," HubSpot, accessed March 20, 2022, https://blog.hubspot.com/blog/tabid/6307/bid/33742/12-Revealing-Charts-to-Help-You-Benchmark-Your-Business-Blogging-Performance-NEW-DATA.aspx.

114 Brian Wallace, "This Week in Infographics #43: From Cars of the Future to Retirement," NowSourcing, January 10, 2013, https://nowsourcing.com/2013/01/10/this-week-in-infographics-from-cars-of-the-future-to-retirement/.

115 "E-Book Market – Growth, Trends, COVID-19 Impact, and Forecasts (2022 – 2027)," Mordor Intelligence, accessed March 21, 2022, https://www.mordorintelligence.com/industry-reports/e-book-market.

116 Stanley McLachlan, "35 Instagram Stats That Matter to Marketers in 2022," Hootsuite, January 18, 2022, https://blog.hootsuite.com/instagram-statistics/.

117 "The Infinite Dial," Edison Research, March 11, 2021, https://www.edisonresearch.com/the-infinite-dial-2021-2/.

118 Stanley McLachlan, "23 YouTube Stats That Matter to Marketers in 2022," Hootsuite, February 14, 2022, https://blog.hootsuite.com/youtube-stats-marketers/.

119 Jessica Bursztynsky, "TikTok Says 1 Billion People Use the App Each Month," CNBC, updated September 27, 2021, https://www.cnbc.com/2021/09/27/tiktok-reaches-1-billion-monthly-users.html.

120 "11th Annual B2B Content Marketing: Benchmarks, Budgets, and Trends," Content Marketing Institute, September 2020, https://con-

tentmarketinginstitute.com/wp-content/uploads/2020/09/b2b-2021-research-final.pdf.

121   Guy Kawasaki, "Readers: Send in Questions for the 'Wise Guy,'" American Express, August 25, 2010, https://www.americanexpress.com/en-us/business/trends-and-insights/articles/readers-send-in-your-questions-for-the-wise-guy-1/.

122   Stephen Babcock, "Baltimore is Number One for Garden Gnomes," Baltimore Fishbowl, April 5, 2017, https://baltimorefishbowl.com/stories/baltimore-number-one-garden-gnomes/.

123   Erin Rodat-Savla, "Social Impact: How a Nonprofit Became a Content Phenom," Content Marketing Institute, February 16, 2015, https://contentmarketinginstitute.com/2015/02/charity-water-nonprofit-content-phenom/.

124   Dominic Gates, "Bellevue Girl Dies After Crash; Her Spirit of Giving Inspires Others," *Seattle Times*, July 23, 2011, https://www.seattletimes.com/business/bellevue-girl-dies-after-crash-her-spirit-of-giving-inspires-others/?msclkid=c48faefda98711ecb492fc3deb0d053d.

125   "Charity's Video Racks Up More Than a Half a Million Views," PR Daily, accessed March 20, 2022, https://www.prdaily.com/awards/social-media-digital-awards/2012/winners/publishers-award/.

126   "We Can Store That," SpareFoot, accessed March 17, 2022, https://about.sparefoot.com.

127   Alexander Harris, "Tech Firms Combine Under Storable Brand Name to Serve Self-Storage Industry," SpareFoot Storage Beat, June 24, 2019, https://www.sparefoot.com/self-storage/news/8148-tech-firms-combine-storable-brand-name-serve-self-storage-industry/.

128   Christopher Calnan, "Young SpareFoot CEO Learned to Hire Industry Veterans," Austin Business Journal, October 14, 2014, https://www.bizjournals.com/austin/blog/techflash/2014/10/young-sparefoot-ceo-learned-to-hire-industry.html.

129   Ryan Dezember, "Got Junk? Self-Storage Investors Hope So," *The Wall Street Journal*, updated December 21, 2018, https://www.wsj.com/articles/got-junk-self-storage-investors-hope-so-11545397201.

130   Mary Ann Azevedo, "Meet LawnStarter, A Profitable Austin-based Startup That Just Raised $10.5M," Crunchbase News, November 12, 2019, https://news.crunchbase.com/news/meet-LawnStarter-a-profitable-austin-based-startup-that-just-raised-10-5m/.

131   Brett Wistrom, "LawnStarter Finds The Grass Is Always Greener With $10.5M In New Funding," *Austin Business Journal*, November 12, 2019,

https://www.bizjournals.com/austin/inno/stories/fundings/2019/11/12/LawnStarter-finds-the-grass-is-always-greener-with.html.

132   Kim Lux, "LawnStarter Acquires Lawn Love," *Lawn & Landscape*, August 3, 2021, https://www.lawnandlandscape.com/article/LawnStarter-acquires-lawn-love/.

133   "About Oracle," Oracle, accessed March 17, 2022, https://www.oracle.com/corporate/.

134   David Gorton, "Eight Companies Owned By Oracle," Investopedia, May 11, 2020, https://www.investopedia.com/articles/insights/081816/top-8-companies-owned-oracle-orcl.asp.

135   Marty Swant, "The World's Most Valuable Brands," *Forbes,* accessed March 20, 2022, https://www.forbes.com/the-worlds-most-valuable-brands/#34f41104119c.

136   "Winning the Content Marketing Battle With Oracle Content Marketing," Relationship One, accessed March 20, 2022, https://www.relationshipone.com/blog/content-marketing-with-oracle-content-marketing/.

137   "Most Powerful Women: Safra Catz," *Fortune* magazine, accessed May 12, 2022, https://fortune.com/most-powerful-women/2021/safra-catz/.

138   "2019 Global Brand Health Report," Hired, accessed March 17, 2022, https://hired.com/page/brand-health-report/top-employer-brands-by-city.

139   Mark Matousek, "Former Tesla Employees Reveal What It's Like To Work With Elon Musk," Business Insider, October 1, 2019, https://www.businessinsider.com/ex-tesla-employees-reveal-what-its-like-work-elon-musk-2019-9.

140   Randy Garn, "Why Is Elon Musk So Successful? It All Comes Down To These 5 Key Personality Traits," Entrepreneur, May 31, 2021, https://www.entrepreneur.com/article/371552.

141   "Elon Musk Asks Twitter Followers If Tesla Should Accept Dogecoin," Al Jazeera, May 11, 2021, https://www.aljazeera.com/economy/2021/5/11/elon-musk-asks-twitter-followers-if-tesla-should-accept-dogecoin.

142   Daniel Ku, "Why Tesla's Social Media Strategy Shows Us It's Time Executives Get Online," PostBeyond by Intuitive, October 14, 2020, https://www.postbeyond.com/blog/tesla-social-media-marketing/.

143   Helen Popkin, "Elon Musk's Twitter Account Is Tesla's $40 Million Marketing Platform. 'Worth It.'," *Forbes,* October 30, 2018, https://www.forbes.com/sites/helenpopkin/2018/10/30/elon-musks-twitter-

account-is-teslas-40-million-marketing-platform-worth-it/?sh=2cf2b-c4b7873.

144 Daniel Ku, "Why Tesla's Social Media Strategy Shows Us It's Time Executives Get Online," PostBeyond by Intuitive, October 14, 2020, https://www.postbeyond.com/blog/tesla-social-media-marketing/.

145 Fred Lambert, "Elon Musk Says No to a New Tesla PR Department, Doesn't Believe in 'Manipulating Public Opinion," Electrek, April 28, 2021, https://electrek.co/2021/04/28/elon-musk-no-new-tesla-pr-department-manipulating-public-opinion/.

146 Aran Ali, "Comparing Tesla's Spending on R&D and Marketing Per Car to Other Automakers," Visual Capitalist, October 11, 2021, https://www.visualcapitalist.com/comparing-teslas-spending-on-rd-and-marketing-per-car-to-other-automakers/.

147 Dustin Christensen, "Are Yeti Coolers Worth the Money?" Territory Supply, August 24, 2021, https://www.territorysupply.com/yeti-coolers-worth-it.

148 YETI, ed. "Our Story." YETI. Accessed August 4, 2022. https://stories.yeti.com/story/our-story.

149 "Company of the Month," National Center for the Middle Market, accessed March 20, 2021, https://www.middlemarketcenter.org/company-of-month/yeti.

150 Tyler Hayzlett, "C-Suite Case Study: The Making of the Yeti Cooler Brand," November 4, 2020, https://c-suitenetwork.com/advisors/c-suite-case-study-the-making-of-the-yeti-cooler-brand/.

151 Ibid.

152 "YETI Dispatch," YETI, accessed March 21, 2022, https://www.yeti.com/en_US/yeti-dispatch.html.

153 "Our Culture Starts with You," Oracle, accessed March 20, 2022, https://www.oracle.com/corporate/careers/culture/who-we-are/.

154 "Oracle Blogs," Oracle Blogs, accessed March 20, 2022, https://blogs.oracle.com/.

155 "Tesla's Mission Statement & Vision Statement: Insights Into the Pioneering Company," Visionary Business Person, accessed March 20, 2022, https://visionarybusinessperson.com/tesla-mission-statement/.

156 Ibid.

157 Ibid.

158 "Most Valuable Brands Within the Automotive Sector Worldwide As of 2021, By Brand Value," Statista, June 2021, https://www.statista.com/statistics/267830/brand-values-of-the-top-10-most-valuable-car-brands/.

159 "Company of the Month," National Center for the Middle Market, accessed March 20, 2021, https://www.middlemarketcenter.org/company-of-month/yeti.

160 "YETI," LinkedIn, accessed May 12, 2022, https://www.linkedin.com/company/yeti/?originalSubdomain=ye.

161 Carolyn Fortuna, "Tesla's 5 Biggest Competitive Advantages," CleanTechnica, July 16, 2020, https://cleantechnica.com/2020/07/16/teslas-5-biggest-competitive-advantages/.

162 Michael Wayland, "GM Says It Will Double Annual Revenue By 2030 to $280 Billion In Digital Push To Be Seen More Like Tesla," CNBC, October 6, 2021, https://www.cnbc.com/2021/10/06/gm-says-it-will-double-annual-revenue-by-2030-to-280-billion-in-digital-push-to-be-seen-more-like-tesla.html.

163 "The 15 Best Coolers Money Can Buy," Gear Patrol, June 15 2022, https://www.gearpatrol.com/outdoors/g39394895/coolers/

164 Sian Babish, "Yeti Review: Do These Top-of-the-Line Coolers and Drinkware Perform Better Than Cheap Alternatives?" *Chicago Tribune,* January 6, 2021, https://www.chicagotribune.com/consumer-reviews/sns-bestreviews-outdoor-yeti-cooler-drinkware-review-20210106-bq5zmgelgjesxjozoqc665d3r4-story.html.

165 Mike Plotnick, "Lessons from a Master Storyteller," Elevate Your Story, August 13, 2019, https://www.elevateyourstory.com/stories/tag/On+the+Road.

166 Steve Hartman, "A Young Girl's Letter to a WWII Veteran was His Most-Prized Possession. The Two Finally Met 12 Years Later," CBS News, September 3, 2021, https://www.cbsnews.com/news/steve-hartman-on-the-road-wwii-veteran-letter/.

167 Sujan Patel, "16 Companies That Are Killing It With Brand-Driven Storytelling," SujanPatel.com, August 20, 2021, https://sujanpatel.com/marketing/7-companies-killing-brand-driven-storytelling/.

168 "The Whole Story Begins with You," Warby Parker, accessed March 20, 2022, https://www.warbyparker.com/buy-a-pair-give-a-pair.

169 "We Have a Couple of Ground Rules at Warby Parker," Warby Parker, accessed March 20, 2022, https://www.warbyparker.com/culture.

170 Sujan Patel, "16 Companies That Are Killing It With Brand-Driven Storytelling," SujanPatel.com, August 20, 2021, https://sujanpatel.com/marketing/7-companies-killing-brand-driven-storytelling/.

171 "How Warby Parker Glasses Are Made," Warby Parker, accessed March 20, 2022, https://www.warbyparker.com/how-our-glasses-are-made.

172 Celinne Da Costa, "3 Reasons Why Brand Storytelling Is The Future Of Marketing," January 31, 2019, https://www.forbes.com/sites/celinnedacosta/2019/01/31/3-reasons-why-brand-storytelling-is-the-future-of-marketing/.

173 "Content Marketing Lesson: The Power of Storytelling," HubSpot Academy, accessed March 20, 2022, https://academy.hubspot.com/lessons/the-power-of-storytelling.

174 "The Art of Story Building," Coursera, accessed March 20, 2022, https://www.coursera.org/lecture/brand-image-high-impact-campaign/the-art-of-story-branding-ZWN2g.

175 Vajahat Tyagi, "Brand Storytelling – Create a Compelling Brand Story," Udemy, updated February 2021, https://www.udemy.com/course/brand-story-telling/.

176 "Content Marketing and Strategy: Brand and Business Growth," Northwestern University, accessed March 20 2022, https://getsmarter.medill.northwestern.edu/presentations/lp/northwestern-university-content-marketing-and-strategy-brand-and-business-growth-online-short-course/.

177 "Brand Storytelling," The University of Texas at Austin Informal Classes, accessed March 20, 2022, https://informal.utexas.edu/classes/brand-storytelling.

178 Johnny Levanier, "What a Brand Persona Is and How to Create One for Your Business," https://99designs.com/blog/marketing-advertising/brand-persona/.

179 "The Power of Storytelling," Bright Innovation, accessed March 17, 2022, https://www.brightinnovation.co.uk/the-power-of-storytelling/.

180 Audrey Schomer, "US Time Spent with Media 2021," eMarketer, May 27, 2021, https://www.emarketer.com/content/us-time-spent-with-media-2021.

181 John Egan, "Report Card: The 14 Most Picturesque High School Campuses in the U.S.," LawnStarter, October 15, 2019, https://www.LawnStarter.com/blog/landscaping/prettiest-high-school-campuses/.

182 Stadium High School in Tacoma WA, "I think we're always first!" Facebook post, accessed March 21, 2022, https://www.facebook.com/plugins/post.php?href=https%3A%2F%2Fwww.facebook.com%2FStadiumHighSchoolInTacomaWA%2Fposts%2F10154641711472169&show_text=true.

183 "B2B Content Marketing 2020," Content Marketing Institute, accessed March 18, 2022, https://contentmarketinginstitute.com/wp-content/uploads/2019/10/2020_B2B_Research_Final.pdf.

184 Jessica Greene, "What's the Best Way to Promote New Content? 41 Marketers Share What Works for Them." Databox, updated December 14, 2021, https://databox.com/the-best-way-to-promote-content.

185 Ibid.

186 John Egan, "The 16 College Football Stadiums With the Best Natural Scenery," LawnStarter, March 11, 2017, www.https://www.lawnstarter.com/blog/environment/best-college-football-stadiums/.

187 John Egan, "The 9 Best College Football Fields With Good Ol' Grass," March 11, 2017, https://www.LawnStarter.com/blog/environment/best-natural-turf-college-football-stadiums/.

188 Jenna Bessemer, "6+ Content Marketing Metrics to Measure Success," Ko Marketing, August 6, 2020, https://komarketing.com/blog/content-marketing-metrics-measure-success/.

189 Tony Stillwell, "Content Marketing Roadmap: The Compass for Your Content Marketing Journey," Divvy HQ, June 12, 2020, https://divvyhq.com/content-marketing/content-marketing-roadmap-the-compass-for-your-content-marketing-journey/.

190 Ibid.

191 Ibid.

192 "12th Annual B2B Marketing: Benchmarks, Budgets, and Trends," Content Marketing Institute/Marketing Profs/ON24, 2022, https://contentmarketinginstitute.com/wp-content/uploads/2021/10/B2B_2022_Research.pdf.

193 Tron Jordheim, "Crazy Tuesday Is Coming! Is Your Self-Storage Facility Prepared?" Inside Self-Storage, May 23, 2012, https://www.insideself-storage.com/crazy-tuesday-coming-your-self-storage-facility-prepared.

194 John Egan, "Workplace Violence May Jump During Return to Work," SHRM, May 27, 2021, https://www.shrm.org/resourcesandtools/hr-topics/employee-relations/pages/workplace-violence-may-jump-during-return-to-work.aspx.

195 John Egan, "CEOs and Workers Don't See Eye to Eye on Mental Health Assistance," SHRM, April 6, 2021, https://www.shrm.org/resourcesandtools/hr-topics/employee-relations/pages/ceos-and-workers-don%E2%80%99t-see-eye-to-eye-on-mental-health.aspx.

196 John Egan and Adam Debrowski, "Coronavirus: Covid and Your Eyes," All About Vision, updated January 2022. https://www.allaboutvision.com/conditions/coronavirus-and-your-eyes/.

197 John Egan and Adam Debrowski, "The COVID-19 Vaccine: Will It Affect Your Vision?" updated September 2021, https://www.allaboutvision.com/en-ca/coronavirus/covid-vaccine-side-effects-vision/.

198 Kim Lux, "LawnStarter Acquires Lawn Love," Lawn & Landscape, August 3, 2021, https://www.lawnandlandscape.com/article/LawnStarter-acquires-lawn-love/.

199 Si Quang Ong, "Evergreen Content: What It Is, Why You Need It and How to Create It," Ahrefs Blog, May 7, 2019, https://ahrefs.com/blog/evergreen-content/.

200 "2022's Best Cities for Remote Workers," LawnStarter, November 15, 2021, https://www.LawnStarter.com/blog/studies/best-worst-us-cities-for-remote-workers/.

201 "2021's Best Cities for Barbecue Lovers," LawnStarter, November 10, 2021, https://www.LawnStarter.com/blog/studies/best-bbq-cities/.

202 Thomas Busson, "The Biggest and Busiest Airports in the US in 2022," ClaimCompass, August 25, 2021, https://www.getservice.com/blog/biggest-busiest-us-airports/.

203 "Remove Barriers, Find Clarity, Exceed Goals", Wrike: A Citrix Company, accessed March 15, 2022, https://www.wrike.com/vm/.

204 Jill Duffy, "Trello Review," PCMag, updated July 13, 2021, https://www.pcmag.com/reviews/trello.

205 "16 Tools to Create Better Images for Your Blog Posts," WPBeginner, November 24, 2016, https://www.wpbeginner.com/showcase/tools-to-create-better-images-for-your-blog-posts/.

206 Alfred Lua, "The 25 Top Social Media Management Tools for Businesses of All Sizes," Buffer Marketing Library, accessed March 21, 2022, https://buffer.com/library/social-media-management-tools/.

207 Ryan McReady, "10 Best Blog Title Generators for 2021," Venngage, May 19, 2021, https://venngage.com/blog/best-blog-title-generators/.

208 Clearscope's website, accessed March 21, 2022, https://www.clearscope.io.

209 Moz's website, accessed March 21, 2022, https://moz.com/.

210 "Global Report Shows Use of Webinars Triples, Driving Digital-First Engagement Across Industries," Business Wire, June 2, 2021, https://www.businesswire.com/news/home/20210602005035/en/Global-Report-Shows-Use-of-Webinars-Triples-Driving-Digital-First-Engagement-Across-Industries.

211 "What Is…Dynamic Content?" Omniconvert, updated March 7, 2022, https://www.omniconvert.com/what-is/dynamic-content/.